Perfect Digital Photos

in a SNAP

The Beginner's Guide to Taking & Making Great Digital Photographs

Click!

IAN PROBERT AND PETER COPE

PHOTOGRAPHS BY MARTIN GISBORNE

ILEX

Click!

First published in the United Kingdom in 2007 by
I L E X
The Old Candlemakers
West Street
Lewes
East Sussex BN7 2NZ
www.ilex-press.com

Copyright © 2007 The Ilex Press Limited

Publisher Alastair Campbell
Creative Director Peter Bridgewater
Editorial Director Tom Mugridge
Art Director Julie Weir
Technical Editor David Asch
Designer Ginny Zeal
Design Assistant Emily Harbison

British Library Cataloguing-in-Publication Data
A catalogue record for this book is available from
the British Library

ISBN 10: 1-905814-18-6

ISBN 13: 978-1-905814-18-3

Printed and bound in China

For more information on this title please visit:
www.web-linked.com/snapuk

Contents

Introduction

Absolutely everyone who has any interest in photography has wished at some point or other that they could make even more of their photo collection.

Have you ever wished that you could instantly share photos of family events with relatives and friends, even if they live far away? Or enhance that faded and creased photo of your great-grandparents to make it look as if it were taken only yesterday? Digital photography makes all this—and much more—possible. Better still, you don't need to be a photography or computer expert to explore and enjoy its wonderful possibilities.

Digital photography is both engaging and empowering. It has reinvigorated a medium that has entertained successive generations for almost two centuries. In fact, it has taken just a few years

to become one of the most popular of contemporary consumer activities—and there are a number of good reasons why.

For some, it is nothing more than the immediacy. Digital cameras give you the ability to see your efforts immediately, in a manner that was once the preserve of those who used Polaroid cameras and film. You can take a photo and enjoy the results instantly. But this immediacy brings other benefits. How many times have you taken a portrait of a group of family or friends only to find, once you've received your photos back from the photo-processing lab, that someone blinked at the crucial time of the exposure? An instant preview makes it possible to check your results and, if necessary, to take another shot.

And there is more to digital photography than the ability to see results in an instant. You can explore new worlds of creativity and enjoy more control

over the image-making process. In conventional photography you could exercise complete control over the taking of photographs, but unless you had both the luxury of a darkroom and the time to use it, you gave up control of processing the photos to a third party. In the photo-processing laboratory, automated equipment produces prints and transparencies that, while technically of the highest quality, often lose or mask the subtle effects you created when taking the shot. Reprints and enlargements suffer the same fate, unless you resort to the expensive luxury of a hand-produced print.

Digital techniques put you in the driver's seat, so to speak, of image creation; you have full control over how your images look. Your computer becomes a digital darkroom that offers not only the convenience of working in daylight, free of the noxious chemicals once essential to image production, but also the opportunity to use tools that allow you to interpret images in any way you wish. Image processing, so long a chore, becomes fun. Creating great images becomes something everyone can do and everyone can enjoy.

But is it really that simple? Taking the first steps in digital photography can seem daunting, especially since you will probably need to learn some new skills. That's where this book comes in. You'll discover that much in the digital photography world represents evolution rather than revolution. If you're an experienced photographer, you'll find digital photography holds few surprises. And if you're new to photography, you'll find that creating compelling images is surprisingly simple.

As most experts will concede, photography and computing are two worlds that tend to generate their own specific jargon. Put them together and you risk creating—however unintentionally—a language that excludes the newcomer.

Turn some ordinary photos into a stunning panorama with some easy digital tricks that anyone can learn.

Part 1 of this book explodes that technological jargon and mystery and explains, using simple English, all the key elements of digital photography. You'll learn here how to make that crucial link between digital camera and computer.

Part 2 looks more closely at getting the best from a digital camera. Many camera—both conventional and digital—boast "point and shoot" simplicity. But once you get to know your camera's controls, you can turn a good photo opportunity into a great one. You'll also learn the best way to photograph different events and different situations, including landscapes and portraits, two of the most popular occasions for camera use. How do you get great memories without being intrusive? And how can you take great night-time shots? Or action shots of sports? Here's how.

Part 3 shows you how to manipulate and enhance your images. You'll discover how, with just a few clicks of the mouse, you can transform a dull photo into a vibrant, colorful one. Or by using a little bit of digital wizardry you can quickly and easily remove that sign that spoils your otherwise perfect landscape composition. You'll discover how you can combine parts of separate photos to create powerful montages of scenes that don't really exist.

What about all those old photos in dusty albums? Can you apply your digital magic to those too? The answer is, of course, yes. Thanks to relatively inexpensive desktop scanners, getting the contents of your old photo albums onto your computer, ready to be manipulated, is just about as simple as using images directly from a digital camera.

This section explains how to get the best results from your scanner and how you can produce prints that are more vibrant than the originals.

Do you know how simple it is to create web-based galleries of your digital masterpieces? **Part 4** looks at how you can place images onto Web pages for the whole world to enjoy, along with other inspirational ideas. How about converting your holiday photos into a CD-based slideshow that anyone can play on their computer or TV? Or make personal greeting cards to celebrate a special event?

The message is clear. In digital photography the only limitation is your imagination. Powerful and memorable images are within your grasp. Read on and find out how.

Whether your photos are landscapes, portraits or snapshots of your latest trip or vacation, a little digital expertise will improve them beyond measure.

Introducing digital photography

Congratulations—you've decided to take the plunge into the digital world. In this chapter we'll introduce you to the world of digital photography, give you a brief rundown of the types of digital cameras you can buy, help you on your way to setting up your camera on your home computer, and preview some of the software features you'll be working with. Soon you'll be on your way to taking your own perfect digital pictures—in a snap!

Click!

Digital pictures

Digital photography has revolutionized the way in which we take, edit, and view photographs. Even if you are a newcomer to the world of digital photography, the chances are that you are already familiar with traditional film cameras, which means you are also familiar with loading film into your camera, waiting for your photographs to be developed, and paying to have enlargements made of your treasured images. Now, with digital photography, you need never do any of this again.

With a digital camera and a home computer, many new opportunities await. Now, you can print out a photograph within minutes of taking it and then email it to friends; create slideshows of your pictures and view them at home; or exhibit images worldwide on your very own web gallery. Or perhaps you will choose to print out your images on an inexpensive inkjet printer. You can correct imperfections, transform colors, or add amazing special effects by using image-editing software such as Adobe Photoshop Elements.

Connect your camera to a home computer and you will never run out of things to do with your digital photographs. Family snapshots can easily be imported into a program such as Adobe's Photoshop Elements, Apple's iPhoto, or Corel's Paint Shop Pro and changed in many different ways.

In iPhoto's *Edit* mode, for example, you can alter the brightness and contrast of your photographs. But this is just the tip of the iceberg—image-editing programs offer you numerous options and unlimited control over your images. In the example above, a simple holiday snap is given an antique look in minutes, using the most basic features of Photoshop Elements.

► **JARGON BUSTER**

What is a digital photograph?
Digital photographs are made up of millions of tiny dots called picture elements or pixels *(see pages 20-21)*. These pixels are stored in your camera or on your computer in binary form—a series of ones and zeros—that the computer can read in the form of machine code and translate into the pictures you see. Fortunately, the digital photographer does not need to have any understanding of machine code to take, edit, or print out pictures.

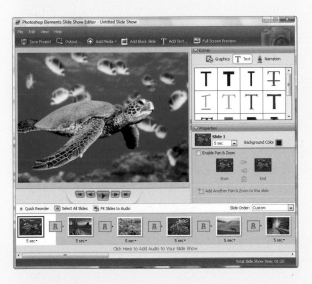

With the click of a button, you can print out your photographs on an affordable inkjet printer, choosing from an assortment of different types of paper.

Alternatively, you may wish to select the email option and have your computer automatically email your photograph to a friend.

You can even take your photographs to be developed in the traditional way and have them printed out or made into bound albums. Or, if you wish to share your work, Photoshop Elements will create slideshows for home display or web galleries for the internet.

The first digital camera

Apple produced the first consumer digital camera in 1992. Known as the QuickTake 100, it had a fixed-focus lens and was able to take up to 32 low-resolution images *(see pages 20–21)* that were stored on a small internal hard drive. These could then be transferred to a computer. Digital cameras have come a long way since then: modern digital cameras are now capable of taking photographs with enormous resolutions, storing their images on removable digital memory cards.

With a home computer and the appropriate image-editing software, you can transform your digital photographs. Here the dull gray in a drab skyline has been replaced with a dazzling deep blue. This type of effect is very easy to achieve— even for the beginner.

Digital cameras

It's easy to understand why digital cameras have become so popular. Digital photography is instant and accessible. You have no film or developing costs, and there is no delay: you take your picture and view it immediately on the small screen on the back of the camera. If you don't like the picture, you simply delete it and take another—and it won't cost you a cent. Many of the main components and features are common to most digital cameras.

Digital versus traditional cameras

Digital cameras are very similar in appearance to traditional cameras. Both types of camera have a lens and a viewfinder—the small window you look through in order to compose the photo. But that's where the resemblance ends. Instead of film, onto which an image is recorded when you press the camera's shutter, a digital camera has a light-sensitive electronic chip (called a Charge Coupled Device, or CCD). When light hits the CCD, an electronic charge is emitted that the camera turns into a digital picture. The images are then usually stored on memory cards *(see pages 18–19)* that slide into special slots in your camera.

(see pages 18–19)

▶ JARGON BUSTER

Megapixels explained

Don't be confused when you see the word megapixel. This refers to the number of pixels *(see pages 20–21)* that your camera uses to record a picture. The least-expensive "entry-level" digital cameras usually have between 1.3 and 3.0 megapixels (million pixels, abbreviated to Mp), while professional digital cameras have at least 6.0 megapixels, with some having as many as 11 megapixels. Generally, more megapixels equals better quality photos. The examples below indicate the size of "photo-quality" pictures you can expect to get with three different megapixel values:

- A *1.3-megapixel* camera will allow you to record and print out a high-quality photograph at up to 4 x 6 inches (10 x 15 cm) in size.

- A *3.0-megapixel* camera will allow you to record and print out a high-quality photograph at up to 8 x 10 inches (20 x 25 cm) in size.

- A *6.0-megapixel* camera will allow you to record and print out a high-quality photograph in excess of 10 x 16 inches (25 x 41 cm) in size.

(see pages 20–21)

DIGITAL CAMERAS

LCD INFORMATION PANEL

Red-eye reduction

Battery charge

Picture resolution

Frames available

LCD information panel

An increasing number of compact digital cameras feature a Liquid Crystal Display (LCD) panel to provide you with information about the camera. This panel provides at-a-glance readouts about the status of the camera's various features, such as how much longer the batteries will last, how many more pictures you can store on the memory card, whether or not the red-eye reduction feature is on, and at what resolution the camera is set.

A standard compact digital camera

Viewfinder
Like traditional compact cameras, most digital cameras have an optical viewfinder, which allows you to compose your shot before taking your picture. Some more expensive digital cameras have an electronic viewfinder, which not only allows you to compose the picture you are taking, but also displays the camera's settings.

Menu button
Pressing this button brings up a range of camera options that are used when taking and reviewing your pictures.

LCD monitor
This small color screen is useful for composing your picture. It also displays information such as shutter speed and exposure settings. In addition, you can use the LCD to review pictures stored inside the camera.

Menu select button
Shift this button left, right, up, or down to navigate through the menus. Press the center to select the highlighted option.

Mode dial
Most compact digital cameras have a mode dial, which, at the most basic level, allows you to take or view ("play back") pictures. On more sophisticated cameras, the mode dial will also offer camera settings for greater creativity.

Zoom button
Many compact digital cameras have lenses that allow you to "zoom" in (or out) on your subject—in other words, they bring the subject "closer" to you. This zoom button also allows you to magnify images when reviewing and editing them on the LCD screen.

Memory card slot
This is where your digital memory cards are housed *(see pages 18–19)*. Some cameras allow you to use more than one type of card.

Function buttons
Most digital cameras have a number of function buttons. These control things such as the flash settings and close-up or landscape photography modes.

Shutter release
As with a traditional camera, when you depress this button, a picture is taken. In some cameras, half-pressing this button automatically focuses the picture and sets the correct exposure.

Built-in flash
Most cameras come with a built-in flash that flashes automatically if there is insufficient light—indoors, for example. More expensive cameras allow you to control the brightness of the flash, as well as to reduce the "red-eye" effect *(see pages 82–83)*.

Click!

Buying a digital camera

Purchasing your first digital camera can be extremely confusing. There is a bewildering array of cameras on the market, from inexpensive models small enough to fit into the palm of your hand, to expensive state-of-the-art digital cameras used by professionals. For this reason, it is best to decide in advance how you intend to use your camera. It may be that a cheaper model will provide all the features you need.

The most important thing to consider when purchasing a digital camera is megapixel size. The greater the megapixel size, the bigger the image the camera will be able to take *(see pages 20–21)*. However, other considerations almost as important as megapixel size are the camera's ease of use, quality of lens, and the availability of accessories and extra photographic features.

There are four main types of digital cameras: compact, intermediate, prosumer, and professional. Note that the majority of photographs in this book were taken with a professional Single Lens Reflex (SLR) digital camera. Digital SLR cameras will be familiar to owners of 35mm film SLR cameras, as they have the same types of features, but in place of the film there is a CCD with a huge megapixel count. Professional cameras range in megapixel size from 6 Mp to 14 Mp; most of these, however, are beyond the price range of casual enthusiasts.

The main types of digital camera

Compact
This type of camera provides a good introduction to digital photography. Its CCDs *(see page 14)* generally start at 3 megapixels but can be as large as 7 or 8 megapixels. This can give reasonable quality prints of up to 11 x 17 in (27 x 43 cm). The lens will usually be of a fixed focal length and will not offer a zoom function. The benefits of a compact are usually size, price, and ease of use. The main limitations will be control and flexibility.

Prosumer
This type of camera is intended for people who wish to develop their photographic skills. As well as a high-quality optical zoom and a 6 to 10 megapixel CCD, it will offer predefined settings for various conditions and a full range of manual controls. It also supports accessories like wide-angle lenses and external flashes.

Intermediate

Taking a step up, this camera will have a similar range of CCD sizes to the compact. The lens quality, however, will be better and feature a moderate zoom feature. Also likely to be included is a range of camera settings for different formats, such as landscape and portrait. This type of camera will generally produce higher quality prints than those of the compact.

Professional

The most advanced cameras offer a wide variety of automatic features, but, even more importantly, allow the user to take manual control of nearly every adjustment, permitting a competent photographer to experiment creatively with settings. These cameras will be built from components of outstanding quality, with many additional accessories available.

Shopper's checklist

- **Number of megapixels**: most cameras will now deliver photo-quality prints. The more megapixels they have, the larger the prints can be, without the need to sacrifice clarity.
- **Optical zoom**: ranges from x2 to x10. The higher the number, the more powerful the zoom. Ignore digital zoom as it gives poor results.
- **Focus**: most compact and intermediate cameras feature automatic focus. If you want more flexibility, ask for a camera with manual override.
- **Modes**: many cameras have different settings for different conditions, such as action, portrait, and landscape. These can help you take better images.
- **Battery life**: check whether the camera takes standard batteries or its own rechargeable kind. If rechargeable, how long does it take to charge, and how long does the charged battery last?
- **Memory card**: the more megabytes the better.

Don't forget to buy...

When you buy a digital camera, consider spending a little more money on useful extras. Most models come with just the bare essentials—a memory card, batteries, manuals, a simple strap, and some connection cables. An extra memory card would be a wise investment *(see pages 18–19)*, and don't forget about the batteries. Some cameras use their own proprietary long-life batteries; others use ordinary AA batteries. Either way, spare batteries will save you from missing out on great pictures when your camera has run out of juice.

It's also worth buying a decent camera case, preferably with some padding. Select one that has sufficient room for your camera, spare batteries, and a second memory card.

Click!

Digital film

Digital cameras store photographs in a different way from traditional film cameras. Instead of using rolls of film that need to be developed, digital cameras store their images on digital memory cards. These come in a variety of shapes, sizes, and specifications. They have the advantage of being reusable—after images have been transferred to a home computer, the digital memory cards can then be cleared and used time and time again.

How much memory?

Each pixel of the digital image contains its own color and brightness information, and in an image with millions of pixels, that soon adds up to a large file. These files are measured in megabytes (Mb). The more megapixels your camera has, the more megabytes you'll need. To use the space more effectively, your digital camera uses a shrinking process, called compression, to pack as many pictures as possible onto the memory card. You can set the strength of this compression (the smaller the file size, the worse the quality, *see pages 42–43*). On a 3 megapixel camera, photos can be compressed to around 1.5Mb and still look good.

Memory cards

The vast majority of digital cameras have one or more slots that allow you to use various types of memory cards. Unfortunately, most cameras come supplied with only a low-capacity memory card—often 16 or 32 Mb. Such a small card may be adequate for a 2 megapixel camera, but if you use a 32 Mb card with a 5 megapixel camera, you will only be able to take a handful of pictures before your card is full.

Some less expensive cameras can only use the camera's built-in memory, which will limit the number of pictures you are able to take. If, for example, you are taking photographs on vacation and you run out of storage space, your only option will be to delete images from your camera.

Buying memory cards

How much memory you need will always depend on your camera and what you are trying to do with it. Remember that the higher the megapixel rating, the more memory each shot will take up. As a result, a 16 Mb memory card might hold 16 or more high-quality photos from a 2 megapixel camera, but very few from a model with a larger CCD. With the cost of memory cards now so low, having even one 256 Mb card as a backup is easily affordable. You can of course build up a collection to make sure you never run out of storage when you're out and about.

Looking after your memory

Memory cards are quite sturdy, but you should try to keep them in a protective case when they are not in the camera. If you need a lot of space for pictures, you should also think about getting two smaller cards rather than one big one. If a card is damaged—accidents can happen to anyone—then it is much better to lose 60 pictures from a 128 Mb card than 120 from a 256 Mb card. That could be a whole vacation!

SD Memory Card

A popular format in recent years, SD memory cards can hold up to 2 Gb (gigabytes) of data on a card the size of a postage stamp. While SD memory cards used to be more expensive than SmartMedia or Compact Flash *(see below)*, there is now no difference in price.

Memory Stick

The Memory Stick method of storing images is available mainly in Sony cameras. In fact, Sony uses the Memory Stick across a range of devices, from cameras to computers and cell phones.

SmartMedia

The SmartMedia card format has been around for many years. While it is a very reliable form of storage, capacity restrictions have meant its popularity has diminished and it is gradually being phased out.

Compact Flash

A Compact Flash card measures approximately 1 inch (2.5 cm) square and comes in a variety of capacities—from the smallest at 8 Mb up to 8 Gb (over 8,000 megabytes). These cards not only come in a variety of capacities, many manufacturers also produce them with different write speeds. The faster the card, the quicker the camera can record the image data; as a result there will be a shorter pause between shots.

XD Picture Card

A recent "digital film" format, XD Picture Card is used in some digital cameras from Fuji and Olympus. Storage capacity ranges from 128Mb up to 2Gb. These cards tend to be slightly more expensive than their SD or Compact Flash equivalents.

Pixels and resolution

A digital photograph is made up of millions of tiny square blocks. These are known as picture elements, or pixels for short. You cannot see individual pixels unless you open up a digital photograph in an image-editing software package and enlarge it using the *Zoom* tool. Each pixel contains important tone and color information, which is required to display a digital photograph on a computer monitor or to print it out.

▶ PICTURE PERFECT

A digital camera's resolution is measured in megapixels (Mp). Generally speaking, the more megapixels your camera has, the better the quality of the picture will be. The larger the camera's CCD *(see page 14)*, the more detail the camera will be able to pick up. A 1 megapixel camera is ideal for simple snaps or for emailing photos to friends, but if you want to print out high-quality images, it is best to use a 3, 4, or 6 megapixel camera. Remember that file sizes get bigger as quality increases.

At normal size, the colors in this photograph appear bright and solid. The curve of the moon fades smoothly into the blue sky.

As we zoom into the photograph, we begin to see pixels appear.

The more we enlarge the photograph, the bigger the pixels get.

Finally, the individual pixels appear as large squares of color. Each of these pixels is made up of a mixture of red, green, and blue.

Resolution

Resolution is what tells your computer monitor or printer how many pixels to display or print per inch of space. Resolution is normally measured in pixels per inch (ppi) or dots per inch (dpi). These are effectively interchangeable within your computer, dpi being traditionally associated with printing. To print at high quality, it is best to output your photographs at a resolution of 300 dpi, so a photograph of 1,200 x 1,800 pixels in size will print out at 4 x 6 inches (10 x 15 cm).

A 6 megapixel image printed at 300 dpi on Letter (A4) sized paper (8½ x 11 inches, or 22 x 28 cm).

A 4 megapixel image printed at 300 dpi on a piece of Letter (A4) paper.

A 3 megapixel image printed at 300 dpi on a piece of Letter (A4) paper.

PIXELS AND RESOLUTION

Buying a computer

In order to take full advantage of your digital camera, you will want a computer that has enough RAM to comfortably run image-editing software and with enough space on the hard drive to store and organize all your images. There are two main types of computers available —the personal computer (PC) and the Apple Macintosh. Both types of computer are perfectly suited for digital photography. Below we suggest the minimum requirements for each system.

In the past it was thought that if you were serious about digital photography, then you needed to buy an Apple computer. However, nowadays there is absolutely no reason why you can't use a Microsoft Windows-based PC. The best applications—such as the image-editing package Adobe Photoshop Elements—are available for both.

There are millions of working components in a home computer, all of them important to its smooth operation. If you are about to purchase a new home computer, however, you need be concerned with only a number of key features.

Hard drive
This is where all the data on your computer is stored, including the computer's operating system, the software needed for editing digital photographs, and, of course, the digital photographs themselves. Hard drives come in many different sizes and are measured in gigabytes (Gb). It is best to purchase a computer with the biggest hard drive you can afford—40 Gb is a suggested minimum. Hard drives can be filled very quickly, especially if you use your computer for other purposes, such as editing digital home movies.

RAM
Your home computer uses Random Access Memory, or RAM, to run its operating system and software. Modern home computers usually have enough built-in RAM for most tasks, but if your computer is running very slowly, then you may need to purchase additional RAM. The ease with which RAM can be installed varies from computer to computer—seek advice from an expert before you install it yourself.

Operating system
On a new system this will be either Microsoft Windows Vista or Macintosh OS X. In terms of usability, there is little difference between the two operating systems, and both are good for digital photographers. Apple computers are supplied with a handy utility to organize your photos called iPhoto, and Windows machines running Vista have the new Windows Photo Gallery.

A typical Windows PC setup

The iMac from Ap

Computer monitor

There are two types of computer monitors available. The first type, the cathode-ray tube (CRT) screen, works much like a standard TV set and is the cheaper of the two options, offering a good, bright image with plenty of color. The second type, the flat panel screen (LCD), is more expensive but can offer better quality and occupy less desk space. Purchase the biggest monitor you can afford—when editing digital photographs you will need as much screen space as you can get. With LCD screens check the pixel dimensions, too, since the display will look good only at the recommended setting. These are usually measurements like 1,024 x 768, or 1,280 x 960. Cathode-ray screens can usually be switched between a number of different settings.

CD-RW or DVD drive

Nearly all computers come equipped with a CD drive that allows you to read a variety of types of CDs, including photo CDs, data CDs, and audio CDs. Most also come with drives that are able to burn (record) CDs—this is very useful for making backups of your photographs. Many models now contain drives on which you can also read and write onto DVDs. These can hold much more data (up to 4.7Gb as standard), which, with the ever-increasing file sizes, make a good archiving solution.

Ports and sockets

If you are buying a new computer, you should find a USB or USB 2 port, the standard for digital cameras. Also look for a "Firewire" (sometimes called IEEE 1394 or iLink) port for faster transfer. Your computer dealer will be able to fit these ports to an older machine too.

CPU and megahertz

When you are working on your digital photos on your computer, there are thousands of calculations going on at any given time. These are made by the Central Processing Unit (CPU) inside your computer. The speed of your CPU is measured in megahertz (MHz) or gigahertz (GHz—1 gigahertz equals 1,000 MHz). The faster the CPU, the more quickly it performs the complicated math, which means that you spend less time waiting when you are adding a great effect to your photo. Windows PCs now exceed 3 gigahertz, although differences in processor technology mean that this doesn't make them three times faster than a 1-gigahertz Apple Macintosh. As a rule of thumb, do not go under the 1-gigahertz mark if you plan to buy a PC. If you are opting for a Mac, aim for a computer with a CPU running at 800 megahertz or more.

Scratch disk

When you are using image-editing software, the image you are working on, and the changes you make to the image, are stored on part of your hard drive called a "scratch disk." It enables you to alter and undo changes without affecting the original image. This is what makes image editing easy and fun, but it does mean you will need a lot of spare space on your hard drive.

Setting up your computer

Most monitors allow you to adjust the brightness, saturation, and other settings using the built-in controls, just as your television remote control does. If the color seems a little wrong, these buttons would seem to be the first things to reach for, but in practice these controls should be set correctly and then left alone. This section is about making sure those settings are just right—but first, here's why you need to do it.

The difference is that, on a television, you adjust the settings so the picture you see is just right and that's all there is to it. The monitor, on the other hand, isn't the only part of the equation when you work digitally. It's more important that the computer knows exactly what color you can see, so that it can make sure the colors look the same when you print that picture, or email it to a friend who will look at it on a different screen, or perhaps their cell phone.

If you adjust your monitor settings, your computer will be as blissfully ignorant of the change as the TV station is when you change the brightness on your television. That's fine, but any other pictures you see on screen—as well as the windows and icons of the computer's operating system—will be affected too. Far better to fix the brightness in the picture itself (as we'll see later in the book) so you can print and send as many copies as you like.

Simple settings

Because there are so many different monitor technologies on the market, achieving consistent color isn't easy. Whatever kind of screen you have, however, the most important thing is to make sure that white looks like white, then make sure there is no bias toward highlight or shadow. The rest will generally fall into place.

This can be done by eye from a suitable color chart, which you can find on the web (for example at http://.photofriday.com/calibrate.php). Life is even easier for Mac users, who just need to press the Calibrate buttton in the *Displays* panel of their System Preferences.

In either case the monitor is adjusted to maximum contrast, then the brightness is adjusted so it's possible to distinguish black from a gray that is about 95% black and, at the other end of the scale, distinguish

Automatic calibration

If you want to ensure that the colors on your monitor are as accurate as possible, you should calibrate using a special device called a colorimeter. This is a relatively expensive solution only needed for those taking their photography very seriously, but the results are excellent. Despite the complicated technology, these devices are very easy to use. You simply plug it into your computer's USB socket and place it over an area of the screen. The included software will then display a series of colors from which the device takes recordings automatically. The program then uses these to form a "profile" of your monitor, which is saved on the computer. Using this it can automatically compensate for any idiosyncrasies it finds.

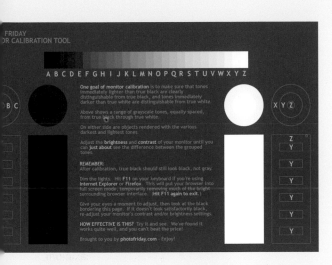

A B C D E F G H I J K L M N O P Q R S T U V W X Y Z

One goal of monitor calibration is to make sure that tones immediately lighter than true black are clearly distinguishable from true black, and tones immediately darker than true white are distinguishable from true white.

Above shows a range of grayscale tones, equally spaced, from true black through true white.

On either side are objects rendered with the various darkest and lightest tones.

Adjust the **brightness** and **contrast** of your monitor until you can **just about** see the difference between the grouped tones.

REMEMBER:
After calibration, true black should still look black, not gray.

Dim the lights. Hit **F11** on your keyboard if you're using **Internet Explorer** or **Firefox**. This will put your browser into full screen mode, temporarily removing much of the bright surrounding browser interface. (**Hit F11 again to exit.**)

Give your eyes a moment to adjust, then look at the black bordering this page. If it doesn't look satisfactorily black, re-adjust your monitor's contrast and/or brightness settings.

HOW EFFECTIVE IS THIS? Try it and see. We've found it works quite well, and you can't beat the price!

Brought to you by **photofriday.com** - Enjoy!

white from 5% gray. That's it, though it's wise to perform this check every few months, especially on older monitors.

Setting your computer's screen resolution

Both PC and Macintosh computer screens have the ability to display images at different resolutions. If you have a Macintosh, you can see this in action by selecting *Displays* in the *System Preferences* panel. Clicking on any of the resolutions in the left-hand menu will change your computer's screen resolution. Doing so will adjust the size of the image that your computer screen displays. This can be useful when dealing with very large images—switching to a high resolution will enable you to see more of the picture.

If you use an LCD flat-panel display, however, you will find that even if more than one resolution is listed in the recommended list, it will only look good at a certain size. This is because of the way this kind of screen works—it is made up of individual pixels rather than displaying from a distance onto a screen.

Connecting camera to computer

Compared to traditional film photography, which requires messy chemicals and a darkroom to print out pictures, digital photography offers ease of use and tremendous flexibility. With a computer and suitable image-editing software, it is possible to totally transform the pictures that you take—and in the comfort of your own home. Before doing so, however, you must transfer your digital photographs to your computer. There are a number of methods of doing this, all of them straightforward and relatively foolproof.

When disaster strikes

Never disconnect a camera from a computer while transferring images. This can cause data corruption and could destroy your photographs. If this should happen to you, there are various software utilities, such as PhotoRescue by software developer DataRescue, that may be able to recover some or all of your missing data.

Fast transfer

Speedy methods of transferring photographs to your computer are available, including USB 2.0 and Firewire 400/800. The latter is faster than USB (the numbers denote the data transfer speeds).

The different connection methods

Most digital cameras come equipped with a USB slot that allows you to connect your camera by USB cable to a USB slot on your computer. On some cameras the slot is easy to find, but on other models it may be hidden behind a movable plastic flap. If your camera is not equipped with a USB slot, you may be able to fit it with a USB adapter.

Connecting your camera to your computer is very easy to do. Simply plug both ends of the cable into their respective USB slots and an icon resembling a hard disk will immediately appear on your desktop. Clicking on this icon will reveal the photographs contained in your camera. These can then be copied over to your computer by dragging them to an appropriate folder. Some types of computer have special photographic software already installed that make this process even easier. Apple's iPhoto, for

example, launches as soon as your camera is connected to your computer—allowing you to automatically transfer photographs into its library. The Windows Vista equivalent, meanwhile, is called Windows Photo Gallery, and performs the same function.

Another option for transferring files to your computer is to use a memory-card reader. These are relatively inexpensive to buy and are often capable of reading several different memory card formats, such as SmartMedia, Compact Flash, or Memory Stick *(see page 19)*. To use a card reader, simply remove the digital memory card from your camera and insert it into the correct slot on the reader. You can transfer images in the same way that you would from your camera, and both Windows Photo Gallery and iPhoto will recognize the images on the card. Whichever connection method you use, you need to start in the same place—with your computer's USB port. See the opposite page for more details.

Although different types of computer may vary in appearance, the method of transferring images from a camera is the same almost universally. Most computers will come equipped with a USB port and most will also have software installed that makes transferring your photographs a straightforward process.

Computer USB port
Simply plug in the USB lead and wait for your camera to connect.

Camera USB port
The camera's USB port is smaller than the USB port in your computer, but works in exactly the same way.

Card reader
Some computers come with built-in card readers. You can also buy readers that plug into your computer's USB port.

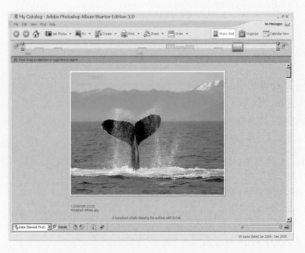

Image-organizing software
Most cameras come with their own image-organizing software. Alternatively, you might prefer to use a more advanced package, such as Adobe Photoshop Elements for PC or iPhoto for Apple Macintosh.

Buying software

After transferring your digital photographs to your computer, the first thing you will want to do is open them up and edit or print them. Most computers today have software preinstalled on the hard drive that allows you to do this. Generally, though, this type of software is very basic with only a limited range of tools. At some point you may want to purchase more sophisticated image-editing software. However, there is a bewildering range of software on the market for you to choose from. Here's a preview of just a few of the programs available.

The beginner will find few image-editing software packages that offer as much value for money as Adobe Photoshop Elements. Although relatively inexpensive, this software package includes many of the features of Adobe Photoshop, the professional image-editing program. Using Adobe Photoshop Elements, it is possible to view, edit, and organize your digital photographs. The program's interface has been designed to suit the novice and provides straightforward step-by-step instructions for most image-editing tasks. The program also allows you to create photomontages, automatically email images to friends, and build web galleries. Adobe Photoshop Elements is available for both PC and Macintosh computers.

Image editing

Version 5.0.2
Photoshop Elements 5.0 is dedicated to our dear teammate Don Cone (1958-2006), whose energy, imagination, and industry helped make this product a reality.

© 1990-2006 Adobe Systems Incorporated. All rights reserved. Adobe, the Adobe logo and Photoshop are either registered trademarks or trademarks of Adobe Systems Incorporated in the United States and/or other countries.

Protected by U.S. Patents 4837613, 5050103, 5146346, 5185818, 5200740, 5233336, 5237313, 5255357, 5546528, 5625711, 5634064, 5729637, 5737599, 5754873, 5781785, 5808623, 5819278, 5819301, 5832530, 5832531, 5835634, 5860074,

Adobe

Adobe Photoshop Elements

Adobe Photoshop Elements is a powerful image-editing program with a wide variety of specialized tools. The program contains many of the features found in its more sophisticated counterpart, Adobe Photoshop, along with simplified, quick-fix tools aimed at the complete novice. The interface is easy to navigate, and built-in step-by-step tutorials cover the majority of common operations.

Adobe Photoshop

Adobe Photoshop is the image-editing choice for most professionals. This program offers just about every image-editing feature you can imagine—and more besides. Having such power at your hands comes at a price, however. Adobe Photoshop can take a long time to master and is far more expensive than packages such as Adobe Photoshop Elements.

Corel Paint Shop Pro

This PC-only package has been on the scene for a long time, offering many of the features of Adobe Photoshop at a fraction of the price. Indeed many users, especially in the Internet graphics field, feel that it has better features for preparing graphics for Internet pages. However, it still lacks some of Photoshop's more advanced new features and is widely felt to be harder to use than the Adobe software.

Other packages

There are a number of alternative image-editing packages on the market worthy of mention, especially for PCs where there is often more choice. Roxio Photosuite and Microsoft Picture are both midrange image-editing software packages with a set of features capable of handling most tasks.

Older software

If you shop around, you may be able to purchase older versions of image-editing software packages such as Adobe Photoshop Elements at greatly reduced prices, but beware—you may discover that the software is unable to work properly on newer computer systems. Additionally, the program may lack some of the features available in more recent versions of the software.

Image organization

As well as buying a package to edit your software, you might want to purchase a program to help you keep track of all your images. Saving a file into folders on your hard drive works fairly well, especially if you remember to give folders sensible names, but using dedicated software can make it even easier to find, print, and back up your images.

Adobe Photoshop Elements Organizer

This was formerly a separate program called Adobe Photoshop Album but is now a part of Elements itself. This program can take images from any source—your hard drive, your camera, or your scanner—and build them into a catalog. You can easily add "tags," such as people's names, to photos and then search for every photo you ever took featuring that one person.

iPhoto

Included with newer Apple computers, iPhoto (shown above) also allows you to keep track of your images and view them in catalog form. It includes a quick retouching tool and a red-eye removal tool for quick changes. iPhoto will also recognize other image-editing programs, such as Photoshop Elements, and link to them seamlessly.

Using imaging software

Chances are that your digital camera came with some form of image-editing software, and despite the fact that this book will concentrate on the latest version of Adobe Photoshop Elements, there is no reason why you cannot use other programs to achieve the same results. Digital imaging is now quite well established, so the way you work in one type of software will be similar to the working practice in another.

If you don't have Adobe Photoshop Elements, check to see if any software has been supplied with your digital camera. It is common for some image-editing software to be included. If so, install the software onto your computer and have a look for the features described here. You may find that individual tools have different names or icons, and that there are other differences in the user interface, but the principles described in the box to the right will remain the same.

▶JARGON BUSTER

User interface

This is the name given to the various menu, tool, and option screens you use to make image adjustments. Different software will have different looking interfaces, but they work in much the same way.

Concepts

Tools

The best way to compare software and its functionality is to look at the tools it offers. In an image-editing package you will use the mouse, rather than the keyboard, to bring about changes to the image. Tools influence the way the mouse behaves, providing you with more possible means to alter your image. For example, a *Text* tool will allow you to click somewhere, then add words to your image, whereas a *Brush* tool will allow you to "paint" directly into an area of the image by clicking with the mouse.

Image correction

Other features of a program can be found tucked away by using the menus. These tend to be the functions that apply to the whole image at once, such as the ability to correct brightness and contrast. Important features to look out for are *Hue/Saturation* and *Levels,* which might be found under an "enhancement" label.

Customization

Because of the complexity of many programs, there are options to open and close some of the windows or toolboxes you are using. This means there is no reason to panic if you don't find what you want right away. It may simply mean you are in a window that is not open at the moment.

File types

Your camera will save a certain type of file, called a JPEG, which is usually compressed *(see page 18).* Image-editing software will give you options to save in other formats. This way it can store more information than just the pixels, including a list of any changes you have made.

Tools

The tools have distinctly different functions, altering the effect of clicking the mouse on the image. Here a *Zoom* tool has been selected.

Tool options

Typically tools can be set with different parameters by a window or *Options Bar*. These affect how the tool works.

Menu Bar

In common with almost all software, image editors allow access to all their functions through a series of menus.

Shortcuts Bar

The program may offer quick access to simple steps like saving files, just like a word processor.

Windows

Called "palettes" by Photoshop. Many programs offer areas displaying additional information and options.

Layers

A feature to look for, but not always available, is the ability to divide the image into layers, which can be moved and edited independently.

Main window

Most of your screen should be taken up with the image you are working on. You can view this at different sizes using a *Zoom* tool, and edit it by applying one of the other tools to it.

Information Bar

Many pieces of software also display useful information along the bottom of the window. Here the present position of the mouse pointer is given in terms of x & y, followed by the size of the image in pixels and the number of colors (the number of colors affects the file size, so it is important to many computer users).

Click!

Adobe Photoshop Elements

If you are new to digital photography and are looking for good-quality image-editing software, you need look no further than Adobe Photoshop Elements. This inexpensive program is very easy to use and includes many of the features and functions available in its professional-level stablemate, Adobe Photoshop.

Adobe Photoshop Elements features a tool set that is standard among many alternative image-editing packages. For this reason, these pages will feature illustrations from Photoshop Elements, but many of the tools described on these pages will have similar or identical counterparts in other image-editing programs such as Paint Shop Pro and Roxio Photosuite.

Starting points

Photoshop Elements makes many of its powerful features available in very user-friendly forms. If the recipes and hints can't help you, the program also comes with comprehensive help files and informative tutorials that you will certainly find useful while you are still learning.

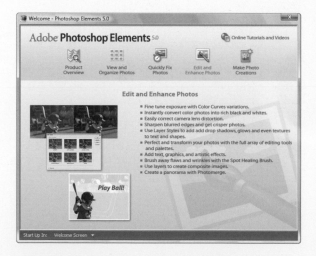

Welcome screen

The welcome screen appears automatically when you launch Adobe Photoshop Elements. This gives you instant access to the most commonly used tasks such as Quick Fixes and Photo Creations. You can also choose whether the program starts up in the Organizer or Editor by default.

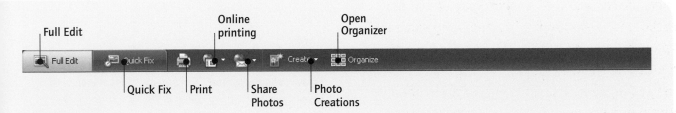

Full Edit

Online printing

Open Organizer

Quick Fix | Print | Share Photos | Photo Creations

Shortcut Bar

From the Shortcut Bar you can switch between the Editor, Quick Fix screen *(see pages 76-79)*, and Organizer. There are also options for e-mailing your photos, ordering prints online, and making slideshows and greetings cards.

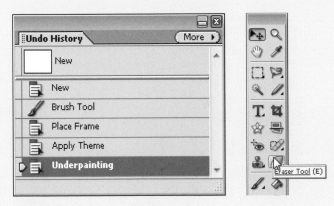

Undo

Elements doesn't punish you for your mistakes. Go to the *Menu Bar* and select *Edit > Undo*. Alternately, use the "Undo" keyboard shortcut. This is Control-Z on a PC, or Apple-Z on an Apple Mac.

Tool tips

If you don't understand an icon or an option, let the pointer hover over it for a few seconds; don't click the icon. The name of the tool or option will appear in a hint box. Clicking on the text opens the *Help Center* on the relevant page.

How to palette

The *Recipe* palette offers beginners access to a number of automated tasks such as *organizing and sharing your photos, cropping and resizing photos* and *simple restoration.* When you select a task, the program will guide you through the process in easy-to-understand steps. Follow the instructions and click the red links if you need Elements to show detailed help.

Help Center

The *Help Center* can be accessed at any time by selecting *Help* from the *Menu Bar*.

continued . . .

Adobe Photoshop Elements—continued

Toolbox

Here you can access all the main tools available in Adobe Photoshop Elements. Each icon displayed in the *Toolbox* represents an individual tool, including drawing and selection tools; *Brush* and *Red-Eye Removal* tools; *Blur* and *Smudge* tools; and *Clone* and *Eyedropper* tools. Click on one to select it, then experiment to see what it does. Note: If the Elements window is maximized and the screen resolution allows, the *Toolbox* appears as a single column.

Tool variations

Some tools, such as the *Marquee* or the *Lasso,* have more than one variation. To see the alternatives, click and hold on the black triangle icon at the bottom-right of the tool icon. The *Marquee,* for instance, has rectangular and elliptical variations.

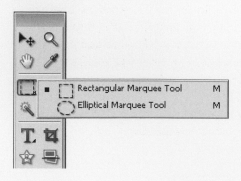

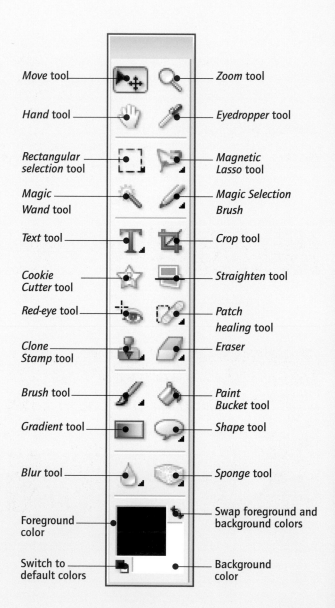

Move tool — Zoom tool

Hand tool — Eyedropper tool

Rectangular selection tool — Magnetic Lasso tool

Magic Wand tool — Magic Selection Brush

Text tool — Crop tool

Cookie Cutter tool — Straighten tool

Red-eye tool — Patch healing tool

Clone Stamp tool — Eraser

Brush tool — Paint Bucket tool

Gradient tool — Shape tool

Blur tool — Sponge tool

Foreground color — Swap foreground and background colors

Switch to default colors — Background color

Tool Options Bar

The Toolbox gives you complete control over the functions of a selected tool. Whenever you select a tool from the Toolbox, an *Option Bar* automatically changes appearance, offering a range of specific controls. If you select the *Paintbrush* tool, for example, the *Options Bar* changes to allow you to adjust brush size, brush opacity, and brush mode. Where there is an arrow, clicking on it will bring up a range of choices. In most cases, you can choose one by clicking on it.

Currently selected tool (*Paint Bucket* tool)

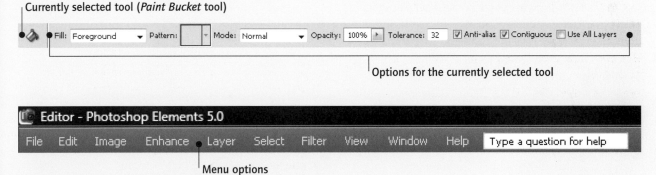

Options for the currently selected tool

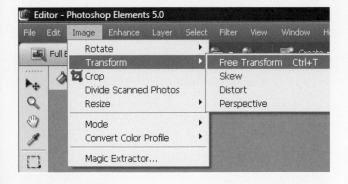

Menu options

Menu Bar

You can also select many of Elements' features from the *Menu Bar* at the top of the screen. This offers a range of options accessed via pull-down menus. Click on the word "Image," for instance, and the *Image* pull-down menu appears. Click on one of the options to select it. If the option has an arrow next to it, then it leads to further options. Later on we will be using menus to make adjustments to our images. When we say *Select Image > Transform > Free Transform*, that means you should click on *Image* in the *Menu Bar*, then *Transform* from the *Edit* pull-down menu, and then *Free Transform* from the next menu that appears.

continued . . .

Adobe Photoshop Elements—continued

Palettes

Photoshop Elements uses a lot of floating windows called "palettes." These contain very specific controls, commands, and options that you will end up using constantly. If you want to get the best out of Photoshop Elements, then you will need to learn how to work with these palettes. They're not hard to access, and it's simple to learn how they work.

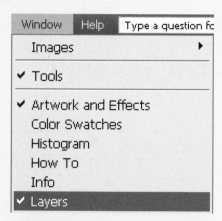

Palette Bin

By default, palettes sit in the *Palette Bin* on the right of the Elements screen. You can selectively hide and show the individual palettes by clicking the arrows to the left of their names. This lets you see the ones you need or use most without too much clutter from the others. You can also open a particular palette by choosing it from the *Window* menu.

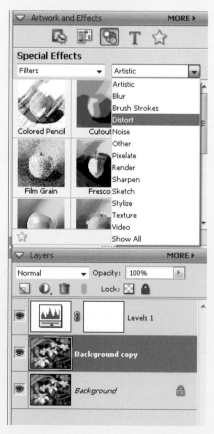

Sliders

Apart from buttons and menus, you will also need to use sliders to choose settings in Elements. The line goes from the minimum to the maximum setting, and you just click, hold, and drag the slider left to go lower, or to the right to go higher. The box above the slider will show the exact setting. If you know exactly what setting you want, you can click inside the box and type in the details.

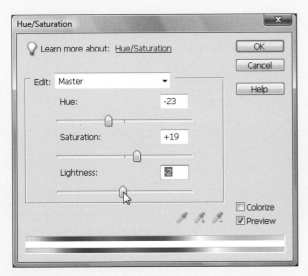

Pop-outs

Elements uses pop-out or pop-up menus in many of its options. Click on an arrow next to a particular command or setting, and a range of different settings will appear. Move the pointer over the pop-up and then release the button over the option that you want.

Moving palettes

Palettes are not trapped in the *Palette Bin*. To move one out, just click on the bar at the top and drag it where you want it to go. You can resize palettes by clicking in the bottom-right corner and dragging that corner in or out. Drag the palette over the well to return it. You can also set the palette to return when the red close button is pressed; this is an option under the palette's *More* menu. If left unchecked, it will close the palette completely.

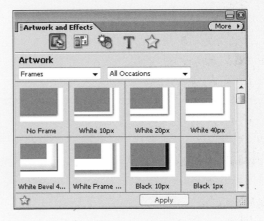

If you have lost a palette and want it back, go to *Window* in the *Menu Bar* and look for the palette in the menu. If there is no checkmark next to the item, click it and the missing palette should reappear.

Using a digital camera

You've bought your digital camera, set up your computer, and now you're ready to go. But first you need to know a little more about how your camera works and what it can do. This chapter explains the basic tools that come with your digital camera and gives you some tips on how to take the best pictures in all sorts of different situations. So, let's get going!

Setting up the camera

Before you use your camera for the first time, spend some time reading the user's manual. Since cameras come with a range of settings that are accessed via the main menu, understanding these settings will allow you to control a range of features—from setting the correct time and date to adjusting the camera's white balance.

One of the first things to do before using a new digital camera is to set the correct time and date. This is important because your camera embeds a record of the time and date when the image was taken inside each photograph. When transferred to your home computer, this information can be read by image-editing software such as Adobe Photoshop Elements or image-cataloging software such as iPhoto. Having the correct time and date embedded in your photographs will help you to store them in chronological order too.

Image numbering

Take care when adjusting the settings in your camera that deal with how images are numbered. In most cases it is advisable to allow your camera to automatically number its images incrementally. In this way, the first picture that you take will be number DSC0001.JPG, the second DSC0002.JPG, and so on. Some cameras allow you to begin the numbering process from scratch each time you insert a memory card. Although this system may be useful if you're working on a particular project, it can also lead to duplication of image numbering—which means that you can end up with several photographs that have the same name.

▶ JARGON BUSTER

Compression settings

Most cameras allow you to set the image size and compression levels independently—this means you can take large pixel-count photographs with high compression, or small pixel-count photographs with low compression. The option that you select is dependent on what you intend to use the photographs for later. Smaller images, such as those intended for use in slide shows or emailing, require a lower pixel count. Larger images, such as those intended for output on an inkjet printer, require a higher pixel count. If you have enough memory, however, there is no need to apply compression at this stage, since it will reduce the quality. You can always compress an image from a high-quality file if you need to email it, but you can't get back information that your camera has never saved.

Autofocus

Many digital cameras have an autofocus mechanism with two main settings: single autofocus and continuous autofocus. In single autofocus mode, the camera will usually not allow you to take a photograph until it has focused upon something within the shot.

In continuous autofocus mode, the camera's mechanism is analyzing the scene constantly, trying to focus upon something in the shot right up to the point when you press the shutter. Single autofocus is the slower method, but it results in more shots that are in focus and will use up less battery power.

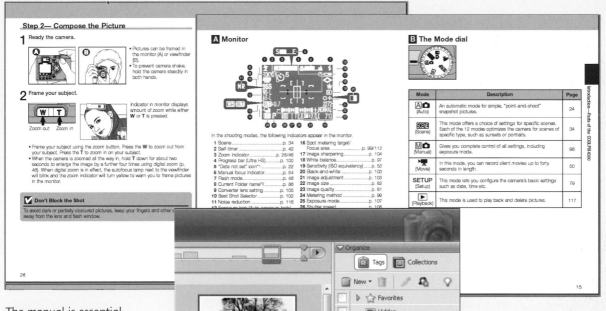

The manual is essential reading when you purchase a new digital camera. It contains information on how to take better pictures, as well as details that are specific to your camera's model.

A screenshot from the *Organizer of Adobe Photoshop Elements* gives an example of the type of information that is automatically stored by your camera within each photograph that you take. As well as image and file size, the time and date of the selected picture and make of camera are also displayed to the bottom left.

Click!

Files and file sizes

Just because an image looks good on your computer screen does not mean it will look good when printed out. This is because the resolution of a computer screen is 72 ppi. To achieve a high-quality printout, the resolution of the image needs to be at least 300 ppi. This can be especially frustrating for beginners, who cannot understand why images that appear just right on their computer screens look blocky or pixelated when they're printed out.

Pixelation occurs when photographs lack the necessary number of pixels. An image 480 x 640 pixels in size will appear perfect when displayed on screen, but that same photograph will look unsatisfactory when printed out. The solution to this problem is to ensure that your photographs are made up of enough pixels. Most cameras allow users to take photographs at different quality settings. A camera's low-quality setting is ideal for displaying photographs on screen, but if you are intending to print them out, it is essential that you use the high-quality setting.

▶ JARGON BUSTER

File sizes

When you increase a digital photograph's resolution, you increase its file size—the price you pay for image quality, and something to remember when planning to use your camera for extended periods. Bigger file sizes mean that fewer images can be stored on your camera's digital memory cards—a 16 Mb card, for example, is only big enough to fit one uncompressed high-quality image from a 5Mp digital camera. For an extended trip or an important once-in-a-lifetime event, it is prudent to keep a stock of the largest memory cards you can afford.

Compression

Digital cameras use a process known as compression to make images smaller. Unfortunately, the more you compress an image, the lower its quality becomes. If you compress a photograph too much, its quality will quickly deteriorate and will render it unusable. The most common file format used is the JPEG format, which is quite flexible and easy to control. JPEG works by looking at groups of pixels and averaging them to a single color. Used carefully, JPEG compression can dramatically reduce file size without compromising quality. Where image quality is the only issue, many digital cameras allow you to save images in an uncompressed RAW or TIFF format.

Compression compared

Image-editing software such as Adobe Photoshop Elements and Corel Paint Shop Pro allows the user to compress photographs in the JPEG format. This table illustrates how adjusting JPEG quality settings reduces file sizes.

JPEG setting	file size (Kb)
no compression	9,216
12	1,856
11	1,283
10	860
9	532
8	367
7	242
6	229
5	167
4	134
3	113
2	103
1	83
0	73

At a typical high-quality JPEG setting of 12, the image is crystal clear and ready for outputting to a printer. File size, however, is big, at almost 2 Mb—almost 27 times larger than the image at its lowest-quality JPEG setting.

At a medium-quality JPEG setting of 8, the image looks less clear. There is a little blurring of the edges. However, even close up, the image appears reasonably clean and in sharp focus. File size, however, has fallen significantly to 367 Kb.

At a low-quality JPEG setting of 4, image quality is far from perfect. There is noticeable blurring around the edges of objects, although there is still some definition in the shadows. This 134 Kb image would still be good enough to email to friends.

At the lowest-quality JPEG compression setting, file size has been dramatically reduced to 83 Kb. However, this comes at a price. Although the photograph doesn't look too bad on screen, you don't have to look too closely to see that almost all of the detail has disappeared and the colors look blocky.

Using a zoom lens

The lens is just as important to a digital camera as it is to a traditional film camera. The lens does the essential job of carrying rays of light into your camera so that its CCD (the light sensor in a digital camera) can record the picture that later appears on your computer monitor. All cameras have a built-in lens that is capable of producing good-quality photographs. Some cameras offer additional features such as a zoom lens.

A zoom lens has multiple focal lengths, which allow many different photographic tasks to be performed. For example, you can look through the camera viewfinder and "zoom" into distant parts of the image—it's like having a pair of binoculars fitted to your camera. Zooms vary in their sophistication and expense. In general, they are not as easy to focus as ordinary lenses, which is why many digital cameras offer an autofocus facility that refocuses after you zoom.

▶ **JARGON BUSTER**

Digital zoom versus optical zoom

Most digital cameras come equipped with built-in zoom features. There are two types of zoom available: digital zoom and optical zoom. Of the two methods, optical zoom offers the better quality but is a more expensive option. Optical zoom uses a lens to magnify images—the same method is also used in traditional film cameras. Digital zoom works differently—it cuts the edges from your image and scales up the middle portion (thereby using a smaller area of the CCD). Unfortunately, the further you digitally zoom into an image, the more the quality decreases. Try to buy a camera with an optical zoom if your budget permits.

Zooming in

Focal length 35mm

Cameras have specifications for their zoom lenses, such as 3x or 4x. This means the camera's lens can zoom in a range that can triple or quadruple. This image was taken with a zoom lens set at a focal length of 35mm.

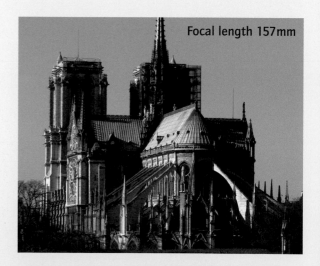

Focal length 157mm

A zoom lens allows the photographer to alter the composition of the shot. At a focal length of 157mm, the building now dominates the scene.

Focal length 75mm

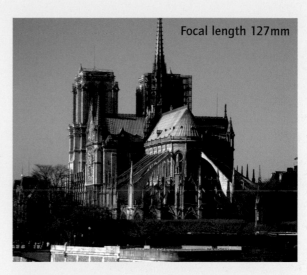

Focal length 127mm

Zoom lenses vary in price and quality. In these images a lens with a range of 35mm to 200mm is being used, which is equivalent to about 6x. Here, the focal length has been increased to 75mm with no loss of image quality.

With the focal length set at 127mm, the building in the distance appears much closer. Detail that was out of range is now clear and well defined.

Focal length 215mm

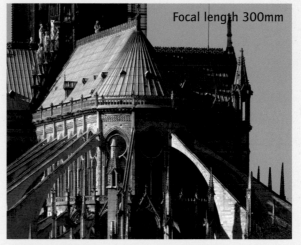

Focal length 300mm

At 215mm the building appears only yards away from the camera. The statues at the base of the roof are now clearly visible.

When the focal length reaches 300mm, the building completely dominates the frame. Without a zoom lens the photographer would have been forced to stand very close to the building to achieve such a viewpoint.

Perfect focus

Focus controls vary from camera to camera. More expensive cameras offer a wide range of features, but compact cameras usually come with a built-in focus that offers limited control. This type of focus control operates by focusing on any object in the central area of the frame. A built-in focus will usually yield good results and is perfectly adequate for most people; professionals, however, prefer to focus their shots manually.

Some cameras have very sophisticated autofocus controls that allow a great deal of creative flexibility. One of the most important features in a digital camera is zone focusing—the ability to select an area in your scene on which to focus. This feature is usually found in your camera's main menu. Zone focusing expands the photographer's creative control. It is possible to create an image in which a foreground object is in focus and the background is blurred, and vice versa.

▶ PICTURE PERFECT

Using manual focus

Manual focus comes into its own when shooting in low-light situations. Because the autofocus on a digital compact camera often struggles to deal with low light, it is wise to switch to manual-focus mode if your camera permits it. In low light you can ensure that everything is in focus by reviewing your image in the playback monitor on your camera. To see more detail, zoom into the image as far as you can. In situations where you have to photograph an object that is moving at high speed, try to prefocus the camera before you take your shot.

Controlling the focus can help to lead the eye into a picture. The sketch of the woman in this photograph is in focus, leaving the artist and the model out of focus.

These two shots illustrate how shifting focus can transform a shot. The first shot has the background statue in focus, revealing ugly graffiti on its chest.

With the focus adjusted accordingly for the second shot, the demon in the foreground is now in focus and the background statue and its graffiti are blurred.

These two images, taken in Paris, illustrate the importance of ensuring that the autofocus locks onto the correct part of the shot. In this picture the autofocus has locked onto the tree in the foreground.

Moving the autofocus indicator slightly allows it to lock onto the historic Notre-Dame cathedral in the background instead.

Shutter speed

One of the most important elements in your digital camera is the shutter, which controls the amount of time that your camera's CCD (light sensor) is exposed to light. The speed of a shutter is measured in fractions of a second, but even minute changes in exposure can make a significant difference to a photograph. Although most compact digital cameras automatically work out the shutter speed for you, learning how to control shutter speed manually opens up endless photographic possibilities.

▶ JARGON BUSTER

How the shutter works

All cameras need light to operate. A shutter works by allowing light to enter the camera for a controlled amount of time. Because no two scenes are lit identically, the speed of the shutter is able to limit the amount of light that your camera receives. For example, when shooting a brightly lit outdoor scene, the shutter need only be open for a very short period. In contrast, when shooting a badly lit scene, the shutter would need to be open for a longer period. A slow shutter speed brings with it its own set of problems, and in most instances it is advisable to use a tripod to avoid camera shake.

▶ PICTURE PERFECT

Waterfalls

Under certain circumstances it is possible to vary the shutter speed with interesting results. When photographing a waterfall or fountain, for example, a long exposure will turn the water into a smooth stream of liquid. Photographing that same waterfall with a fast shutter speed will capture a split second in time and will look very different. Using a slow shutter speed will soften your photographs—a very effective method for indicating movement and speed.

At very high shutter speed, an object's motion is frozen. This water sculpture at the Long Beach Museum of Art was taken with a shutter speed of 1/4000 of a second.

This shot of a fountain in Portugal has an extremely slow shutter speed of 1 second. Here the water has been transformed into streaks of light.

Fast-moving objects

These two images illustrate the shutter's ability to freeze the action. With a shutter speed of 1/45 second, the car is a little blurry as it speeds by.

This second shot was taken at 1/250 second. The car in the foreground is traveling at roughly the same speed as in the first picture, but this time it is completely sharp.

Sporting events

Freezing the action with a high shutter speed records detail not seen by the naked eye. This rider in the Tour de France was moving at 35 mph. With a shutter speed of 1/2,500, he is frozen in time.

A moderate shutter speed will blur fast-moving parts of the image, but retain sharpness in the more static areas. This picture of San Jose Sharks' Jonathon Cheechoo at practice was shot at 1/180 of a second. At that speed his head is steady, but his hands and stick are moving rapidly.

Aperture settings

The aperture is an adjustable opening that allows light to pass through your camera's lens. Along with the shutter, it is responsible for controlling the amount of light to which your camera's CCD (light sensor) is exposed. The bigger the aperture, the more light will be let into the camera. Because learning to control your camera's aperture settings takes some practice, most compact digital cameras automatically work them out for you.

Aperture settings are measured in f-stops such as f/8 or f/2.8. This number is calculated by dividing the focal length of the lens by the diameter of the aperture. A wide aperture setting lets more light in and requires a faster shutter speed. A small aperture setting lets less light in and therefore needs a slower shutter speed.

▶ JARGON BUSTER

Depth of field

As well as controlling light, the aperture has another important function—it can transform the appearance of a photograph. When a camera's aperture setting changes, the depth of field of the image is also altered. Depth of field is a term used to describe the area that will be in focus between two distances from the lens. By manipulating the depth of field, it is possible to achieve a range of effects. With a shallow depth of field, for example, the subject of a portrait can be in focus with the background blurred. Alternatively, a deeper depth of field keeps both foreground and background in focus. That is why the hole in a pinhole camera is small enough to put everything into focus.

This shot by Graham Cooper is a fine example of aperture affecting depth of field. The aperture setting was f/2.8. Used with a long focal-length zoom, this created a very shallow depth of field. Note that the camel's nose is in focus, but the eyes are blurred.

Aperture and depth of field

This series of three photographs illustrates the extent to which aperture and depth of field can affect an image.

Here, the aperture has a wide setting of f/3.2, leaving the tree fully in focus and the background indistinct.

Shifting the aperture to f/8 retains sharpness in the tree, but the background is not as unfocused.

The aperture has been closed right down to f/22. The background is not sharp, but it is much clearer.

Notice how depth of field affects this shot. Only the central section of the wire is in sharp focus.

Framing

Composition is of paramount importance in photography. Even when correctly exposed, a photograph can still look terrible if the composition is wrong. Compositional theory has been developed by artists over the centuries—the rules they follow apply equally to photography. What you choose to leave out of a picture is sometimes just as important as what you put in.

FRAMING

When taking photographs, beginners often make the mistake of placing their subject directly in the center of the frame. This may seem like a natural thing to do, but the results are usually less than satisfactory: objects and people may appear lost in the picture. Good composition can be achieved by shifting the viewpoint and mentally arranging the shot before it is taken. Digital cameras have the advantage over traditional film cameras because the LCD screen allows you to see a good representation of the composition of the image, so you know in advance what your photograph will look like. You also have a second opportunity to recompose your shot later with your computer.

The Golden Section

Although there are a host of techniques to aid composition, the most popular has been around for hundreds of years. The Rule of Thirds—or the Golden Section—was used by Leonardo da Vinci back in the 15th century. It works by dividing the image vertically and horizontally into three equal sections. Where the lines intersect are natural points of interest. If you position key elements of your image along these points, you will find that your photograph comes to life.

The woman in this image is positioned along one of the three key verticals of the Golden Section. Her head is very close to one of the four intersections. Because of this, the scene is far more dramatic than it would have been if the subject had been positioned in the center of the frame.

Tricks of the trade

Use of diagonals can help to lead the eye into the picture, giving the image greater depth and making it more interesting. Look around and you will see that diagonals occur everywhere in nature.

The train lines head off into the distance, turning an ordinary picture into a dramatic image. The rails become an arrow pointing the eye toward the mountains in the distance.

Another strong diagonal, this time at an approximate 30-degree angle, is used to balance a gentle seascape.

Composing with a zoom lens

Try using your built-in zoom lens to help compose a shot—zooming in even a little can completely transform a composition. It can also help you to get rid of unwanted elements such as passers-by accidentally getting into the shot.

In this shot the subject is totally lost in the frame.

After zooming in very slightly, the subject fits into the frame much more comfortably.

White balance

White balance is the method used by digital cameras to ensure that the colors in your picture look as natural as possible. This is an area where digital photography has a definite advantage over traditional photography. Whereas film cameras require a lot of extra equipment to make adjustments in white balance, digital cameras have built-in white-balance controls. Additional adjustments in white balance can also be made on a home computer.

During the day, a bare white wall will subtly change color. In the morning it is blue-white; by midday it has become pure white; in the late evening it is orange-white; and under artificial lighting conditions it is a yellow color. This shift occurs because of changes in color temperature caused by the light. Compact cameras do a good job of automatically dealing with white balance, but under extreme conditions you may have to experiment with the range of manual settings included in your camera's menu options to get the desired result.

▶ **PICTURE PERFECT**

Creative use of white balance

Your camera's white-balance controls can be used creatively to correct color change. If, for example, you wish to make a picture appear warmer, select your camera's "Cloudy" white-balance setting. Similarly, if you wish to make a photograph appear cold, select your camera's "Tungsten Bulb" white-balance setting. Experimenting with different white-balance settings in different situations can achieve a wide range of results.

WHITE BALANCE

White point

These examples illustrate how much this setting affects the color in your picture. All six photos were shot in the same lighting conditions, but with different white-balance settings.

Tungsten bulb

Fluorescent lighting

Sunlight

The camera's automatic white-balance correction has done a good, but not perfect, job of compensating for conditions. Automatic sensors are often fooled by images that do not have a good mix of colors.

Cloudy conditions

Some cameras come with presets for certain lighting conditions. The camera knows exactly what sort of light to compensate for, so it can be more accurate.

Sensitivity settings

The International Standards Organization (ISO) assigns a rating to the film used in traditional cameras, which defines for the user the film's particular sensitivity to light. A lower ISO rating such as 100 means that more light is needed to expose the image correctly than a higher ISO rating such as 800. Although a digital camera does not use film, it nevertheless offers some control over the sensitivity of its CCD *(see page 14)* comparable to that of film cameras.

Using different ISO settings

If you are in a well-lit environment, a fast shutter speed will enable you to take good-quality photographs. If the light levels are lower, however, you will have to lower your shutter speed to achieve acceptable results, although this may cause camera shake. As an alternative, you can increase the ISO setting on your camera. This will make the camera's CCD more sensitive, shortening the length of the shutter speed. There is, however, a drawback to using high ISO settings.

Noise

Using a high ISO rating has a tendency to generate "noise" in photographs. Noise appears as small spots on an image. These spots are usually white in color and no bigger than a single pixel in size. This phenomenon occurs most frequently in long exposures but can often be eradicated on a home computer using an image-editing program such as Adobe Photoshop Elements. This, however, can be a tedious exercise and does not always guarantee satisfactory results. An image taken with a long exposure will usually include one or two bright areas that can bleed into surrounding pixels. These may be impossible to fix on a computer.

Many cameras offer an auto ISO feature that will increase the ISO sensitivity as light levels drop. On occasion, you may wish to switch off this feature and manually select the ISO setting, since manufacturers' settings are often too general to be helpful in all situations. If the camera is mounted on a tripod, a high ISO rating is unnecessary because the camera will not shake during a long exposure, so using a manual ISO setting is best.

In the shot below, taken in a stadium, the light was too low to allow for a fast shutter speed to freeze the action at a low ISO setting. To get a suitable shutter speed, the ISO was increased to 800, and although the resulting shot was quite successful, some "noise" is visible in the highly enlarged detail.

ISO settings

This image was photographed with three separate ISO settings; the exposure settings were the same for each shot.

ISO 400

At the camera's middle setting, the colors and contrast have changed considerably. Now that the camera is more sensitive to light, the shot is more washed out, and noise can be seen in some areas.

ISO 100

At the camera's lowest ISO setting, the image appears clear with realistic-looking colors.

ISO 800

At the camera's highest ISO setting, all detail on the foliage has been lost. There is even more noise in the darker areas of the image.

The flash

Most digital cameras come equipped with a built-in flash, which allows you to illuminate a dark or badly lit scene that would otherwise be impossible to photograph. As with traditional film cameras, if used correctly, flash can be an invaluable tool. In the wrong hands, however, flash can ruin a photograph.

▶ **PICTURE PERFECT**

A built-in flash is ideal for photographing indoor events such as parties. When doing so, try to ensure that your subjects do not stand too close to a wall, since this will produce hard shadows. Because your camera's built-in flash will struggle in low-light situations, remember, too, not to stand too close to the subject, as the flash will obliterate any detail. Finally, try experimenting with the flash settings in your camera's menu. Most cameras have a range of settings, which can help prevent your subjects from being overexposed in the bright light of the flash.

Using flash at night
Using a flash at night is very useful in outdoor locations. As long as you are close to the subject, the flash is ideal for illuminating the foreground. Some cameras even offer special nighttime shooting modes that automatically calculate the correct exposure and flash intensity settings.

This shot of a man standing against a bridge in the late evening would not have been possible without flash, since the differences in exposure readings for the subject and the sunset were simply too great. Without a flash, it would have been possible to photograph the sunset *or* the man in the foreground—but not both.

Using flash in daylight

Using a flash in daylight can often help you to avoid taking photographs in which the foreground subjects appear too dark. A flash can be especially useful when you are photographing people or objects in front of a bright background. This is known as a fill-in flash.

This picture was taken during the day, without flash, producing poor results. The man in the foreground appears far too dark.

This shot was taken during the day with a fill-in flash. The result is a much better picture—the man is now correctly exposed, as is the background.

How a flash works

A built-in flash is powered by your camera's main batteries. When you depress your camera's shutter, a device within the camera's circuitry releases stored-up energy. This results in a very bright burst of light, usually lasting no longer than a split second. This burst of bright light helps to illuminate the scene.

Compared to larger external flashes, a built-in flash actually produces very little light. An important thing to remember is that, beyond a few feet, the built-in flash in most cameras is largely ineffective. For this reason it is best to avoid using a flash when photographing large objects such as buildings.

Click!

Advanced camera features

Nowadays, even less expensive digital cameras come with a wide range of advanced features. These include photography mode, noise reduction, and autobracketing. Some cameras even allow you to record small movies that you can edit and play on your home computer. Here we take a look at some of the most useful of those advanced camera features, whose controls can usually be accessed in the main menu of your camera.

Photography mode

Some cameras have a dial that enables you to select various custom photography modes such as portrait, landscape, sports, and night scenes. When you select one of these modes, your camera will automatically calculate the best exposure, shutter speed, and aperture size for the type of photograph you wish to take. This can be extremely useful, for example, when you are photographing fast-moving action scenes outdoors, and you have limited opportunity to adjust your camera settings manually.

Noise reduction

Noise is a common problem when taking digital photographs at night or in low-light situations. Noise appears on digital images as small dots that are usually white in color *(see page 56)*. Many cameras use various techniques to remove unwanted noise; these include double exposures and a built-in noise reduction mode. A nighttime scene *(below right)* was taken with a long exposure. Note the amount of noise in the image, appearing in the photograph as white and red spots. The same shot *(below left)* with in-camera noise reduction activated has enabled the camera to remove much of the noise.

Autobracketing

This feature automatically shoots three consecutive frames of the same image at different exposure settings. It is useful in difficult lighting conditions, allowing you to transfer all three images to your computer later and select the one with the best exposure. This nighttime shot *(below left)* has been underexposed and is of poor quality. Had the photograph been taken in brightly lit conditions, however, a slightly underexposed shot could have been better. The second shot of the series *(below right)* is correctly exposed, but the lighting in the scene is still not bright enough. The third shot *(bottom)* is slightly overexposed but has picked up far more detail and light in the dim conditions than the previous versions. It is now ready for printing or further improvement using image-editing software.

Continuous shooting mode

Selecting this mode allows you to shoot up to five photographs in very quick succession. This is particularly useful when photographing moving objects. More expensive digital cameras enable you to take even more than five photographs.

Sharpness setting

Some cameras offer a range of sharpness settings that affect how your photographs are taken. In general, these settings are identified as: Hard, which is best for shooting buildings or text; Normal, suitable for normal photography; and Soft, best used for photographing people.

Multiexposure setting

Using this setting allows you to superimpose several images onto one frame. To do this, you will need a tripod. Remember that multiexposure can also be achieved using image-editing software.

External flash

Some digital cameras are fitted with "hot shoes" that enable you to fit and use an external flash.

In-camera image editing

Many cameras allow you to trim your photographs in-camera. Although this sounds like a useful feature, it should be avoided. Trimming photographs in-camera reduces the resolution of the image, which means that you may later find yourself unable to print the photograph to a satisfactory standard.

Digital printing

Many cameras allow you to save your images in the Digital Print Order Format, or DPOF. This is useful if you do not have access to a home computer or inkjet printer. With your images saved in a DPOF, you can then take your camera's digital memory cards to a photo-developing facility and have them print out the images for you.

Camera tricks

Many digital cameras come with special built-in camera tricks such as Sepia Tone and the ability to capture small video clips. Some features can be very useful if you do not own a computer. But, in general, it is better to use image-editing software such as Adobe Photoshop Elements or Corel Paint Shop Pro on your computer to add special effects to your photographs. The reason for this is simple—in-camera special effects transform the image stored in your camera without making a copy of the original. In contrast, your computer allows you to experiment with copies of your photographs while still preserving your original image.

Special Effects

In general, there is no in-camera special effect that cannot be duplicated or improved by using image-editing software. For this reason it is always advisable to shoot your photographs in color and with no in-camera special effects. If you do this, you can make as many copies of the photograph as you like without losing the original.

Email-ready cameras

Some cameras have the useful ability to create a second version of a picture that is email-ready. An email-ready camera makes a copy of a particular image and reduces it in size so that it can be easily emailed.

Shooting video clips

Some cameras can shoot small video clips. While the quality does not match that of dedicated video cameras, this feature can be great fun to use and an ideal way of recording memorable events. Different cameras capture video in different ways, but most record their footage in Apple's QuickTime format at a low resolution of 320 x 240 pixels. Some cameras allow you to record sound but most will allow you only to capture a maximum of 30 seconds' worth of footage. Like ordinary digital images, video clips are stored on your camera's memory cards. Clips can be transferred onto your computer and edited using Windows Movie Maker (for PC users) or Apple's iMovie (if you have a Macintosh computer).

In-camera or in-computer effects?

A digital photograph of a beautiful yellow Indian motorcycle basking in the California sunshine. Once you have taken a shot such as this, you can experiment with it in all kinds of ways using image-editing software; for example, adding soft focus, or changing the colors.

This shot could have been created in-camera using a Sepia Tone setting. It was, however, created from the full-color original image, using Adobe Photoshop Elements after the original image had been saved.

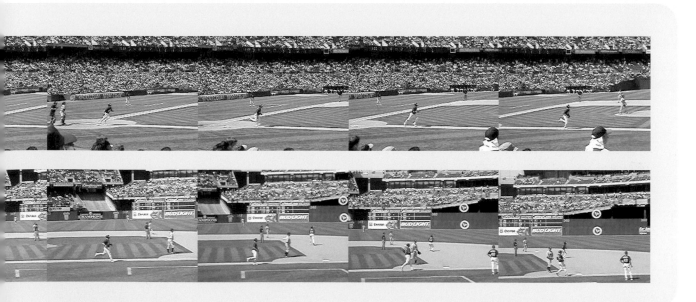

Click!

Perfect portraits

Shooting portraits is one of the most satisfying aspects of photography. From capturing a family member's likeness to taking group portraits outdoors or in a studio, there are many different areas of portrait photography to explore. With a little effort, even the cheapest compact digital camera is capable of producing a memorable portrait shot.

Capturing the character and style of a person is not as hard to do as it might appear—but it is something that requires thought. Everyone has a wide range of expressions and body movements that are unique to them. It is important to get to know what these expressions are and how to inspire them in your subject. For most portraiture, it is better to move slightly away from the subject and use the zoom facility on your camera. This saves your subject from feeling uncomfortable in front of the lens, but beware—if you move too far away, lens distortion will make your subject's face look fatter.

Wide aperture shots

Use a wide aperture setting to keep the subject in focus while blurring the background. With no background to focus upon, the subject becomes dominant in the frame.

Composition

An unusual composition can make a portrait more exciting. The head of the woman in this image occupies only the bottom third of the frame, allowing the viewer also to take in the speed and movement of the background.

Unusual viewpoints

You do not need to stand directly in front of a subject to take an interesting portrait. Changing your viewpoint can transform a subject. Seen from above, the subject of this photograph appears flattened within the cool background.

Element of surprise

Surprising a subject is often a good way of getting them to relax. In contrast to the forced grins often seen in formal portrait shots, this subject's smile is obviously genuine.

Using a zoom lens

The camera was some distance from the subject when this photograph was taken. Note that the face of the woman was made fatter because of lens distortion caused by zooming in too closely. Never stray too far away from your subject.

Click!

Perfect landscapes

Landscapes can be one of the hardest subjects to photograph, but here's one area where your digital camera offers a number of advantages over traditional film cameras. First, the LCD screen on your camera allows you to view scenes instantly without having to trudge all the way back to the studio. Second, digital editing software is particularly useful for manipulating or enhancing landscape shots.

When photographing a landscape, it is essential that you decide which element of the scene you most want to capture. If the land is your priority, you need to ensure that the horizon is positioned one-third from the top of the frame. Alternatively, if the sky is to be photographed, the horizon should be positioned one-third from the bottom of the frame. This broad use of thirds should ensure the success of your landscape shots.

▶ PICTURE PERFECT

When photographing seascapes, be careful that your camera's autoexposure does not overcompensate for the reflections of light coming from the water. If at all possible, use a manual exposure setting and point your camera at a midtone detail such as sand. This will help ensure that no detail is lost.

Landscape compositions

Each of these five examples demonstrates an effective way to catch certain striking features of a strong landscape shot.

Some 15–20 minutes after the sun has disappeared, the sky will suddenly erupt into deep reds, pinks, and oranges. However, the lack of bright sunlight will mean you'll be working with a slow shutter speed. Use a tripod to avoid camera shake.

Using the Rule of Thirds, in this shot the horizon is situated one-third from the bottom of the frame, allowing the dramatic sky to dominate.

Again the Rule of Thirds has been followed, but this time greater prominence has been given to the mountains, which dominate the lower two-thirds of the picture.

Using a narrow aperture setting ensures a good depth of field and keeps the whole shot in focus, allowing the viewer to see all of the colorful detail in the scene.

Use of scale can help convey the immensity of nature. The flowers in the foreground of this shot give the viewer a visual indication of how far away the mountains are.

Perfect action shots

Action photography can include sports, adventure, and vacation activities—in fact, almost any situation in which the subject is moving. By definition, action photography captures some sort of action and, therefore, movement. Capturing movement can be very difficult—even for seasoned professional photographers. To capture an object that is moving, a photographer has to be prepared to accept that images will often be blurred or out of focus. In fact, deliberately blurring a picture when taking action photographs can often enhance the feeling of energy and movement and may make your final image work better.

▶ PICTURE PERFECT

Introducing movement into the shot

Blurring an object is the simplest way of suggesting movement in an action photograph. Using a slow shutter speed is usually best for doing this. As you prepare to photograph a subject that is moving past the camera, try to track it in your viewfinder by pivoting your body until you are ready to take the shot. In this way, you will keep the moving subject in sharp focus, but the background will be blurred behind it.

Motion
These images show the different results of the blurring effect that motion often brings. In each case it helps tell the story rather than detract from the quality.

If you track a comparatively slow movement, like this handball player's jump, your subject will stay in sharp focus. Note that here, only the ball and the slightly blurred background suggest any movement.

If you are working with a lot of light, such as that reflected from the ice here, select a faster exposure setting to get a better action shot. Except for the hands and stick, the movement is frozen, and the background is slightly blurred.

To keep the subject looking sharp and blur the background, turn to follow the movement of the subject as it passes the camera. Move in a smooth sequence, avoiding jerkiness as you press the shutter.

With the camera mounted on a tripod, a slower exposure has ensured that the background remains in focus. In fact, the only parts of the photograph that are moving are the subject's head and arms. You could ask your subject to move their body in other ways if you preferred.

The slow exposure used in this photograph has turned the moving balls into ghostly wisps of color. If you want a "ghosted" image, ensure the subject is well lit and the camera steady, and use a long exposure.

Click!

Perfect night shots

Taking pictures at night can create spectacular images. To do so, however, it is necessary to think about your subject beforehand and consider how you would like it to look in the photograph. Cities are particularly beautiful when photographed at night. The bright neon lights of the buildings and roads can work very well when taken with a slow shutter speed setting. Moving light sources such as cars will produce eerie streaks of light that dramatically illuminate your photographs.

When not to use flash

In some nighttime situations, the flash is more of a hindrance than a help. When shooting objects, buildings, or people at a distance, turn the flash off and use a longer exposure instead. Most built-in flashes in compact cameras are weak, so using a flash at night will illuminate only a subject close to the camera. Everything else in the shot will be too dark to be seen clearly *(see pages 58–59)*. If you use a long exposure, more of the scene will be visible. The only drawback is that any movement in the scene will cause blurring—although this can be a great effect in itself.

▶ **PICTURE PERFECT**

If your camera has a self-timer feature, this is very useful when shooting at night. Even with a tripod, the camera will wobble slightly when you press the shutter. A self-timer can prevent this from happening by allowing you to press the shutter several seconds before the shot is taken.

Instant tripods

A tripod will help when you are taking long exposures, but if you don't have one with you, it is possible to use any stable surface to balance your camera. Books, stones, trashcans, vehicles, or soda cans can all be used to prop up your camera and can make good makeshift tripods.

By using a long exposure, this ferris wheel becomes a blurred mass of moving color.

In the darkness, this building is ablaze with light. A long exposure allowed the camera to capture the straight lines of the blue lasers reaching into the sky.

The carved figures on this ship are illuminated by a very dim light source, yet appear bright and detailed. That's because a very long exposure was used. If a tripod had not been used, this shot would have been blurred beyond recognition.

Christmas lights in the harbor take on a magical quality in another long exposure.

A detail of the Eiffel Tower in all its glory—a single searchlight cuts a diagonal line across the sky in this long exposure.

The digital darkroom

Even the best professional photographers don't always take the perfect picture. The beauty of digital photography is that if your picture doesn't turn out exactly how you wanted, you can make it right—sometimes with just the click of a button. In this section we profile the most common problems that can occur and show you the best fixes for each situation. In addition, we present ideas for using photos in new ways, tips on special effects, solutions for storage, plus darkroom secrets straight from the pros.

Exposure

Many digital cameras are able to automatically work out your photograph's correct exposure for you. Most of the time this will result in good-quality images that are well exposed and have strong contrast. On some occasions, however, your camera will produce less-than-perfect results. When this happens, you can use any image-editing software package to easily correct or adjust the exposure of your photographs.

The golden rule when correcting exposure is that it is easier to brighten a dark image than it is to darken a bright image. That's because the white parts of a digital photograph contain virtually no usable information in the pixels. For this reason, it is far better that an image be slightly underexposed—this will give your image-editing software something to work with when you come to correct or adjust your photograph's exposure.

▶ PICTURE PERFECT

Quick Fixes

Most image-editing software programs have functions that allow you to adjust exposure. These functions vary in sophistication from simple brightness and contrast controls to automatic exposure correction tools available in programs such as Adobe Photoshop Elements. This popular image-editing package includes useful features such as *Shadow/Highlight and Quick Fix*; these make it easy to correct a variety of common exposure problems.

Underexposure

This shot of a tumbledown but picturesque shack shows all the typical signs of underexposure, including flat, gloomy colors and a lack of contrast and definition. Below are several ways of dealing with this.

1 The easiest approach is to switch to *Quick Fix* mode by clicking the *Quick Fix* tab on the *Shortcut Bar*. This gives you access to all the most useful adjustment tools on one screen.

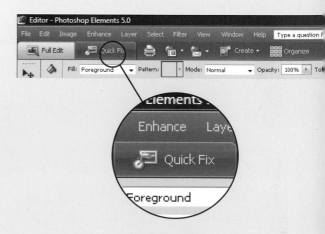

Quick Fix button

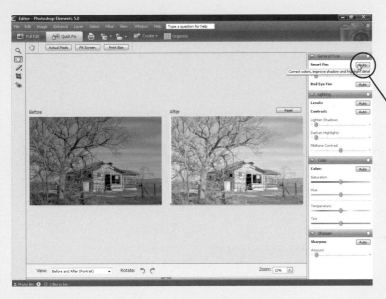

2 Begin by applying *Smart Fix*. Click the *Auto* button at the top of the palette on the right of the screen. This function automatically optimizes the shadows, highlights, and colors of the image. This can also be applied manually with the slider below.

3 For this image, and for most shots that are over- or underexposed, *Smart Fix* will work well. Sometimes, however, it can overcompensate. You may, for example, like the colors slightly less saturated, in which case you can use the *Auto Contrast* option. For stronger colors and tones, try *Auto Levels*. There is also the option to adjust the image manually.

4 The result here is much more vibrant. The great thing about using the *Quick Fix* mode is that you can experiment as much as you like. Try different adjustments and and click *Reset* if you make a mistake. To apply the changes, simply switch back to Edit mode.

continued . . .

EXPOSURE ●

Exposure—continued

Brightness

While the *Quick Fix* tool's *Auto Contrast* and *Auto Levels* options will solve most exposure problems, another of the Lighting adjustments which is well worth a look, particularly for shots taken indoors, is the *Shadow/Highlight* adjustment. This can be used to add extra artificial lighting to a dull scene and bring it back to life.

1 This hotel's lavish re-creation of the canals of Venice is one of the highlights of a visit to Las Vegas, but an underexposed photograph fails to capture the building's full glory. To correct this, the image is opened in Adobe Photoshop Elements.

2 The program's *Quick Fix* tool will automatically correct many of the common exposure problems you will encounter. It offers a range of corrections that can alter brightness, color, and the sharpness of the image. Here, the image has been brightened using the *Lighten Shadows* adjustment. You can preview the changes alongside the original by selecting one of the *Before and After* views from the menu at the bottom of the screen.

Shadows/Highlights

Learn more about: Shadows/Highlights

OK

Cancel

Lighten Shadows: 25 %

☑ Preview

Darken Highlights: 0 %

Midtone Contrast: 0 %

3 Alternatively, you can make the same adjustment by selecting *Enhance > Adjust Lighting > **Shadows/Highlights.*** This enables you to adjust the shadows, highlights, and contrast as in Step 2, but without switching to *Quick Fix* mode..

4 The result is a much improved image, which does a far better job of capturing the subtle lighting and details of the scene.

Overexposure

Auto Levels is just as effective at dealing with overexposure, as in this washed-out shot of the Golden Gate Bridge. After 30 seconds with the *Quick Fix* tool, this dull, low-contrast image has a lot more punch and color.

▽ Lighting

Levels: Auto

Contrast: Auto

Lighten Shadows

– ――――――――― +

Darken Highlights

– ――――――――― +

Midtone Contrast

– ――――――――― +

Contrast

Contrast is the number of shades, from dark to light, contained in a picture. One of the most common problems that digital photographers encounter is a lack of contrast in their images. Generally, a good photograph will contain all shades, from black to white. There are some occasions, however, when low contrast can add atmosphere to a photograph. With a computer and some image-editing software, you can control the contrast in your photographs in any way you choose.

There are a number of ways of correcting or adjusting the contrast in a digital photograph. By far the most straightforward method is to use *Levels* or the *Brightness/ Contrast* controls of your software. These controls are both available under *Adjustments* in the *Image* menu and work in different ways. Selecting the *Brightness/Contrast* control brings up a panel with sliders that you can drag with your mouse to adjust the brightness and contrast. The *Levels* control is slightly more complicated to use—this allows you to adjust the individual red, green, and blue color channels in your photograph. *Levels* is a very powerful tool to use—you can find out more about its capabilities on pages 96–97.

Improving contrast

before

after

1 Sadly, the *Quick Fix* auto options don't work every time. This shot, for example, clearly needs some contrast correction. *Auto Contrast* would be the first option for most people, and from the thumbnail it appears to have worked.

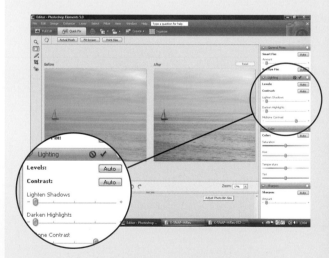

3 Sometimes it's best to do things by eye. This time, concentrate on the Midtone Contrast setting. Click and drag the slider slowly toward the right until you get the right effect.

2 Click *OK*, however, and look at the corrected shot. There is more contrast, but the effect is slightly overdone. You can go too dark and moody! To undo the *Auto Contrast*, select *Edit > **Undo***, then click on the *Quick Fix* button to return to the options.

4 This new shot might not have quite the same impact, but it is a calmer, more lifelike result. As always, experiment with the *Quick Fix* palette and find what works for your photo. If you don't like what happens, you can always *Undo* it.

Auto Contrast

The *Auto Contrast* quick fix solves many contrast problems at a stroke, such as this bleached view of San Francisco. Select *Brightness* from the *Adjustment Category* section, *Auto Contrast* as the adjustment type, then click *Apply*. Simple.

Removing color casts

Digital photography gives the user enormous control over color. With a home computer and the correct image-editing software, it is possible to alter individual colors, transform overall color schemes, correct color casts, and add subtle tints to images to enhance the overall feel of a photograph. More importantly, this degree of flexibility comes with tools that enable you to repair images that would otherwise be unusable.

Color cast is one of the most common problems in color photography. It is caused by variations in lighting and is visible as a discoloration that can make the whole photograph look odd. Images taken under fluorescent lights will, for example, appear on a computer screen with a green tint; similarly, images taken under tungsten lights will have an orange tint. Thankfully, these are both problems that can be fixed on your home computer.

Color correction

Most image-editing software packages have automatic controls that make it easy to correct color casts. These controls are adequate for many tasks but lack the necessary sophistication for more demanding jobs. This is when controls such as *Hue/Saturation* and *Color Balance* come into their own. These tools allow you to change the color value of selected parts or whole images. If, for example, a photograph has a red color cast, this can be altered by adding more green to the image—the opposite color on the color wheel. Similarly, a yellow color cast can be fixed by adding more purple to the scene—once again, opposite on the color wheel.

The *Remove Color Cast* tool

Remove color casts with the Remove Color Cast tool (*Enhance > Adjust Color > **Remove Color Cast***). Simply click an area of the image that should either black, white, or gray.

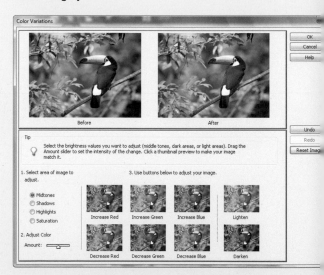

To quickly add color tones or remove them from an image, use the *Color Variations* tool (*Enhance > Adjust Color > **Color Variations***). Click on the buttons to add or subtract red, green, or blue in the shot, and to lighten or darken it at the same time.

Many dull portraits can be improved with an additional dash of orange. This compensates for the colder blue tones and adds some extra warmth to the picture.

1 This yellow color cast can be dealt with using the *Color Cast Correction* tool, or by increasing the red in *Color Variations*.

2 We're not finished yet, however. Some color adjustments can sap the contrast from an image. We need to put the definition back in.

3 Selecting *Enhance* > **Auto Levels** from the *Menu Bar* soon puts the sparkle back.

Red eye

Red eye can be a very big problem for photographers when taking portrait shots. It occurs when light from a camera's flash strikes a subject's retina and illuminates the mass of blood vessels present there. Under normal conditions the retina appears black, but occasionally this phenomenon will ruin your photograph by turning a subject's eyes a ghoulish red color.

Thankfully, there are ways of preventing red eye. The simplest is to move the flash to the side of the camera and alter the angle at which the light strikes the subject's eyes—ideal if your camera can use an external flash, but in compact digital cameras this might not be possible. Cheaper cameras usually come equipped with built-in flashes that sit directly above the camera lens, so it is sometimes impossible to avoid red eye. Many cameras feature a red-eye flash mode, which works by firing the flash twice. The first flash makes the subject's pupils contract; a second brighter flash moments later is then used to illuminate the scene. If you use this feature, warn your subject: photographs can be ruined when the subject moves away after the initial flash, assuming that the shot has been taken.

RED EYE

▶ PICTURE PERFECT

Sometimes it is impossible to avoid red eye when taking photographs. This is the time when image-editing software comes into its own. Programs such as Adobe Photoshop allow you to eradicate red eye by selecting the affected pixels and recoloring them black. Adobe Photoshop Elements and Apple's iPhoto offer an even easier solution: both programs come equipped with special tools that vastly simplify the removal of red eye.

The *Red Eye Removal* tool

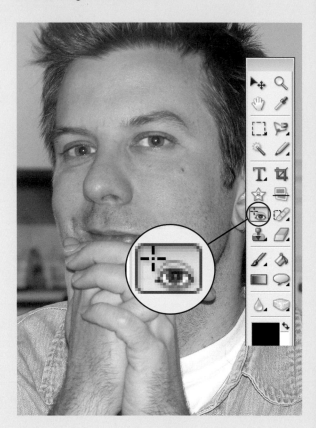

1 A cheerful portrait has been ruined by red eye. To fix, use Adobe Photoshop Elements and select the *Red Eye Removal* tool from the Toolbox.

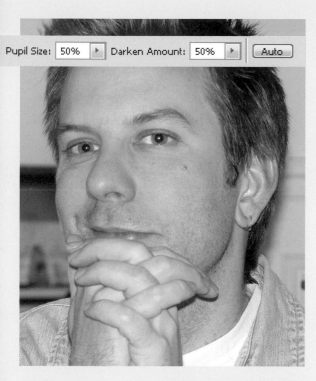

Pupil Size: 50% ▶ Darken Amount: 50% ▶ [Auto]

2 The first and quickest way to use the tool is with its auto function. Simply click the *Auto* button in the *Options Bar*. Elements will analyze the image and fix any instances of red eye it finds.

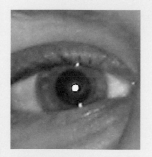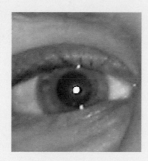

3 The automatic function works well but is not always completely accurate. The tool can also be used selectively: click the cursor on the red pupil and Elements will fix it.

Removing red eye is just as easy in Apple's iPhoto. In *Edit* view, select the *Red Eye* tool and draw a square around the area that you want to change. Now click the same tool once again and the red eye is removed. Repeat the same process for the other eye. You can also use Elements' *Quick Fix* mode or, for complete automation, you can set the *Organizer* to detect and remove red eye as your images are downloaded from the camera.

Sharpening

Even the best photographers cannot guarantee razor-sharp images every time. No matter how experienced a photographer you are, low light or other tricky autofocusing conditions can lead to slightly fuzzy images. This is a common problem with digital cameras. Fortunately, most image-editing packages include a standard sharpening feature that allows you to adjust a slightly blurred image and bring it into sharper focus.

SHARPENING

Unsharp Mask

The most popular digital sharpening feature is called *Unsharp Mask*. Creating an unsharp mask is the process of hiding, or masking, the portions of the image that are not sharp—or, in other words, are unsharp. *Unsharp Mask* is standard in most image-editing programs, including Adobe Photoshop, Adobe Photoshop Elements, and Corel Paint Shop Pro. *Unsharp Mask* operates in a similar way in each program and is easy to control when you have mastered the basics.

You may notice similar commands, such as *Sharpen*, *Sharpen Edges* and/or various other sharpening options, but professionals almost always use the *Unsharp Mask*.

▶ PICTURE PERFECT

Sharpening for the Web

An image that looks sharp on screen may not appear as sharp when you finally print it out. It's a good idea to make a second copy of any image that you want to print out and sharpen it differently from any image that you want to use in an on-screen presentation, such as putting it on the Web.

Unsharp Mask at work

This close-up shows the *Unsharp Mask* at work. The image on the left is the original. In the center, an *Amount* of 150% and a *Radius* of 4 has been applied; a *Threshold* of 10 has been used to keep the skin tones smooth. The image to the right has an *Amount* of 200% and no *Threshold*; the results look harsh—your subject will not thank you for her emphasized wrinkles and uneven skin.

Controlling the Unsharp Mask

In Photoshop and Photoshop Elements, the *Unsharp Mask* has three controls that affect the image in different ways. Once you understand how these controls work, you will find it much easier to sharpen your images.

Amount simply controls the intensity of the sharpening effect. The higher the percentage, the sharper the effect.

Radius is a little trickier. The *Unsharp Mask* function acts on clusters of pixels, enhancing the contrast between each pixel in that cluster. Altering the *Radius* makes those clusters bigger or smaller. Making the clusters bigger increases the overall sharpening effect dictated by the *Amount* setting. As a rule, the smaller your image, the less *Radius* you should use—usually setting the *Radius* between 1 and 4 is ideal.

Threshold is the most complicated of the three controls. This allows you to control the range of pixels that will be sharpened. A high *Threshold* setting applies the filter only to pixels that vary greatly in brightness, such as the edges of objects. A low *Threshold* setting applies the filter to pixels of similar brightness, such as skin tones. Experiment with these settings to fully understand their implications.

Perfect sharpening

1 Before you sharpen, start by zooming in to "actual pixel" size. Check that a value of 100% is shown in the bar at the bottom of the window. You can quickly zoom in to 100% by selecting *View > Actual Pixels*. If you are not zoomed in to 100%, it is impossible to gauge the effects of the filter.

2 In Photoshop Elements 5.0, the *Unsharp Mask* moved from its old location. It is now found at the bottom of the *Enhance* menu (not the *Filter* menu, as in previous versions).

3 When working with the *Unsharp Mask*, uncheck *Preview* in the dialog box (click on the little check-mark under *OK*). This way, you can see the original in its present state and use the preview in the filter itself for fine-tuning.

4 Every image will need a different adjustment. Begin with an *Amount* of around 200%, then move the *Radius* up or down depending on the size of the image. A setting of 4 can be ideal for a higher-resolution image. You can then go back to the *Amount* setting and increase or decrease until the edges that you want to sharpen look sharp enough. If there are signs of oversharpening in areas—the skin, for example—then it is time to bring the *Threshold* setting into play, shifting it steadily upward until the skin looks smooth again.

Click!

Softening and blurring

Most of the time you will want your pictures to be perfectly sharp. However, there are occasions when selectively blurring or softening part of an image can add impact. There are many types of pictures where you can successfully apply softening, including portraits, landscapes, and sports shots. These photographs all have one thing in common—they often work better when you blur the less important parts of the image and draw attention to the subject of the picture.

▶ PICTURE PERFECT

Professional portrait photographers always aim to get the eyes of a subject totally sharp and in perfect focus, while leaving the rest of the face, neck, and shoulders slightly out of focus. Because this effect requires special lenses and fine control, it is almost impossible to achieve using most digital cameras. You can, however, simulate the effect with the method described on the right.

Selective blurring

1 This is the original shot. As you can see, the main figure looks slightly lost against the background. We can fix this using the Photoshop Elements *Blur* tool.

4 Begin to gently brush some blur onto the background object. You can also blur the foreground to really push that feeling of depth.

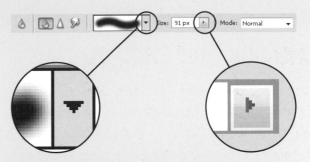

2 The idea here is to give the image greater depth by selectively blurring parts of it. Select the *Blur* tool (with a teardrop icon) from the *Toolbox*.

3 Go up to the *Options Bar* and select a reasonably large, soft-edged brush. Select the type of brush by clicking on the arrow next to the brushstroke button on the left, and the size by clicking on the arrow next to the *Size* box. When you move the mouse pointer back over your image, it will turn into the circular brush. If it looks too large or too small to work with, go back to the *Options Bar* and select a more appropriate size.

5 When brushing between areas of fine detail, you will need a smaller brush. You should, for example, reduce the size of the brush to work between the twigs of the bushes, so that you blur all of the background but leave the bushes in sharp focus. Work carefully and adjust the brush size up and down until you have blurred all you need to.

6 The photo now has greater impact, with more emphasis on the subject. To better capture the idea of desert heat with this particular image, use the *Brightness/Contrast* tool *(see pages 78–79)* to brighten the sand and give the impression of heat. Adding +20 to each setting gives the desired effect.

Cropping and straightening

Most image-editing software packages include cropping and straightening tools. Using the Crop tool in Photoshop Elements gives you a second chance to compose a photograph and remove unwanted elements such as power lines. The tool has an equally important role in straightening images—you can, for example, use this tool to adjust pictures in which the horizon is not level.

The *Crop* tool is very easy to use. First, select the tool and click in the top-left corner of the area you want to keep. Then, holding down the mouse button, drag the mouse down and to the right until you have the correct area captured in the rectangular box that appears. This box is called a marquee. When satisfied with your selection, hit *Return* and the tool will delete the rest of the image. This process has many useful applications and comes with the additional advantage of allowing you to rotate your selection and straighten it. Be careful, because cropping means that you delete actual pixels from your photograph; always be sure to keep a copy of your original file.

▶ PICTURE PERFECT

Straightening an image
The easiest way to straighten an image is with the *Straighten* tool. Position the cursor on one side of the horizon line. Click and drag the guide across to the opposite side of the photo, following the horizon's angle. When you release the mouse, Elements will automatically straighten the image. Different options are available from the *Options Bar* which determine how the empty space is removed after the image has been rotated.

Quality control
When using the *Crop* tool, remember that the file you are left with will be smaller than the original. An image that has been cropped will no longer print at its previous size. This usually makes little difference when making small crops, but if you crop away too much of the image, it may become too small to print out properly.

This shot was taken at sunset on the beach in Long Beach, California. In the original shot the horizon is not level, but after some judicious cropping, it is now perfectly straight.

Creative use of the *Crop* tool

1 Select the *Crop* tool from the *Toolbox*. The *Crop* tool usually has this icon, which resembles the two "L"s that traditional film photographers used to work out a cropping position.

2 With the *Crop* tool it is possible to select a predefined cropping size. This is very useful when cropping an image to print to a particular size and resolution.

3 This shot is too straight to be interesting. Use the *Crop* tool to select a part of the image. Click and drag diagonally to create your cropped area.

4 Move the crop cursor outside the selected area and it turns into the curved rotate cursor with arrows at either end. Click and drag up or down, or left or right, and the selected area will rotate.

5 Rotate the selection until the viewpoint is more interesting. Click the tick at the right-hand end of the *Options Bar* when you are happy. This strong diagonal composition is now much more dynamic than the original.

Vanishing tricks—cloning

The *Clone* tool—or *Rubber Stamp*, as it is sometimes called—is one of the most useful features of Photoshop Elements. This extremely flexible tool allows you to make corrections to problematic images and create amazing special effects. The *Clone* tool works by copying pixels from one part of an image and using that part to correct imperfections such as stray hairs or scratches on another, visually similar, part. This process is known as sampling.

With the *Clone* tool you can, for example, remove wrinkles and make your subject look years younger. If you wanted to, you could even give your subject three eyes and an extra head! The *Clone* tool allows you to use the sampled pixels as digital paint. If, for example, you wish to remove an unsightly pimple on a subject's face, you can use the *Clone* tool to sample pixels from an unblemished area of skin and then "paint" these pixels over the imperfection to hide it. The *Clone* tool operates in the same way as any other brush—there are controls for size, softness, and opacity that you can adjust at any time as you work.

To use the *Clone* tool, first move the tool over to the area of the picture that you wish to sample. To remove a stray airplane from a blue sky, you would, for example, choose to sample an area of clear blue sky. Press the *Alt* key, then click to select this source—you can then begin painting with the *Clone* tool as you would with any other type of brush. Experiment with this tool and you will notice a small cross that follows your brush as you paint. This is the source point that you selected—as the brush moves, the small cross follows its movements, constantly resampling the image.

Using the *Clone* tool

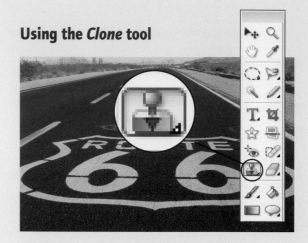

1 If construction workers had not left marks that spoiled the pattern, this photograph of Route 66 would make an ideal cover for a road-trip scrapbook. This is a job for the *Clone* tool.

The first step is to locate the *Clone* tool in your software. You can find it on the main Adobe Photoshop Elements *Toolbox*.

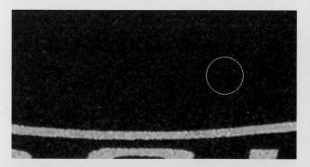

3 Using the *Tool Options Bar*, select a suitable brush with which to do your painting. Soft edges ensure that the cloned material blends in smoothly with the rest of the picture; you also need to adjust the brush to the right size. Brush over the sign, but watch out for odd patterns caused by straight copying. If these appear, hover over the area with the mouse and click quickly on it to create random spots of texture. This should remove any noticeable patterns.

2 Next, zoom into the part of the picture you want to work on and pick a source point that shares the same tones and textures as the area you want to replace. Once you have identified the source area you wish to copy, move the cursor over it while holding down the *Alt* key and clicking the mouse. Here, an area of black road has been selected.

4 The completed image with all the imperfections cloned away.

Cloning tips

• Selecting the source point is the key to good cloning. The source point is linked to the painting part of the Clone tool. If you paint to the left, the Clone tool will sample pixels to the left of the source point. If you move up, the source point will also move up. If, for example, you are attempting to remove a blemish from a subject's forehead, do not select a point below the eye—you may finish up accidentally creating a third eye!

• Look at the element of your photograph that you are trying to remove. Then look at the area immediately surrounding it. Visualize what the area would look like without the offending object. Then search your image for an area that contains the tone, color, and texture you want.

• Watch out for shadows or strange color tones in the areas you are cloning to and from. If these end up out of place, they can spoil the final effect.

• Make sure that the brush settings for your *Clone* tool are adjusted to give the brush a soft edge. This will produce a smoother blend and help prevent your image from appearing pixelated.

Click!

Selections

Selecting parts of a photo is an essential part of image editing. By making a selection of the right area before trying to change anything, you can protect other areas from being changed. Selections can also be moved around and even copied and pasted into completely different images—great for montages and for moving items around in a photo. There are different selection tools, each with their own strengths, but they all create the same thing: a selection.

SELECTIONS

A selection shows up in your image as an animated black and white dotted line, an effect sometimes called "marching ants." When a selection is active, anything you do—from painting through to color balance and filter work—will change only the selected area. Spend a little time getting your selection just right, and you can go wild without worrying about messing up the surrounding areas of the photo. Once you have made a selection, you can use any selection tool to grab it and move it around. This means you can use the same selection in different areas over and over.

Feathering

Feathering is the process of creating soft-edged selections and can be the key to achieving a truly professional result. Feathering allows a gentle fading out of the selection border. The *Feather* feature in the *Options Bar* changes how the tools will work for the next use, whereas the *Feather* item in the *Select* menu will soften the edges of an existing selection. Feathered selections are useful for montaging in different layers *(see Layers on pages 98–103)*.

Methods of selection

You can find all of the selection tools in the main Photoshop Elements *Toolbox*. At first you will be ableto see only the standard *Rectangular Marquee* tooland the *Polygonal Lasso*. Click and hold on the button to see the other *Marquee* or *Lasso* options.

Lasso tools

For irregular selections, the *Lasso* tools work better. With the *Lasso* tool, click and hold to draw around the area you want, then let go to select it. This takes a steady hand. The *Polygonal Lasso* tool is easier to use. Just click around the image to build the selection point by point. The *Magnetic Lasso* is a smart version of the last tool. It automatically creates selections around the edge of an object in the image, but you can click to add "anchor points" around difficult corners.

Marquee tools

The *Marquee* selection tool is the simplest selection tool. This can be either a rectangle or an oval. It works much like the *Crop* tool. Click in one corner of the area you want to select, and drag the *Marquee* out until it encloses the area you want to select. Click outside the selection area if you need to start again.

Selection Brush

The *Selection Brush* is both fun and easy to use. Just paint over the area you want to select, and hold down the *Alt* key to switch to deselecting with the brush. Try changing the softness to get a feathered selection, or change the brush size to pick smaller or larger parts of the image. You will need a small brush if you are making fine selections.

Magic Wand

The *Magic Wand* is perfect for selecting similar shades and colors. Click on an area, and all connected similar shades will be selected. Change the *Tolerance* setting in the *Options Bar* to select a tighter or broader range, and uncheck the *Contiguous* option to select all similar colors in the image, wherever they are.

Adding and subtracting

Normally, a selection tool will automatically "forget" any selection that's already been made. However, you can add multiple selections together, building up a big complex selection in small parts, and also carve away at selections to deselect unwanted areas. In the *Options Bar* there are four buttons for controlling this: they are *New Selection, Add to Selection, Subtract from Selection*, and *Intersect with Selection*. You can see them running from left to right in the *Options Bar*.

Advanced color controls

Sometimes what's needed to make an image look just the way you want is more than just a tweak with the *Color Cast* tool or picking some generalized *Variations* options. If you want to do something seriously creative, such as making the sky green and the sea purple, look instead to the *Hue/Saturation* and *Replace Color* features, found inside the *Adjust Color* list in the *Enhance* menu in Photoshop Elements. With these you can alter colors wholesale, colorize the image like a tinted black and white photo, or even change specific color ranges within an image while leaving others alone.

When changing colors using either of these methods, do remember to zoom in and out and look over your image carefully. While you're using the *Hue/Saturation* or *Replace Color* windows, you can't switch tools using the Tools palette, but you can use the keyboard shortcuts. Press *Control-Space* (*Apple-Space* on the Macintosh) to zoom in, and press *Control-Alt-Space* to zoom out. Press the space bar to grab the image and move it around within the window as you need to.

The hue-changing part of the *Hue/Saturation* controls works by taking the whole color range of the image and sliding it around the color wheel—shown in the window as a horizontal strip of color—so that the colors in the image are remapped to different hues. Saturation boosts or reduces the color without changing the shading, but the *Lightness* slider tends to make images duller or wash them out. Use *Brightness/Contrast* or *Levels* from the *Enhance* menu's *Adjust Brightness/Contrast* options.

Replace Color

First, let's use *Replace Color* to change the color of a glass of beer. If the glass sits against a neutral background, it's not too hard. Select *Enhance > Adjust Color > Replace Color*, then click on the *Eyedropper* button and click on a patch of beer inside the glass.

The display in the *Replace Color* window shows which part of the image will be changed: white is completely affected, gray less so, and black not at all. If not all the beer is selected, move the *Fuzziness* slider to the right or use *Add To Sample* and click on other parts of the glass.

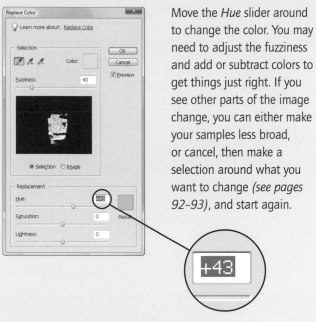

Move the *Hue* slider around to change the color. You may need to adjust the fuzziness and add or subtract colors to get things just right. If you see other parts of the image change, you can either make your samples less broad, or cancel, then make a selection around what you want to change *(see pages 92-93)*, and start again.

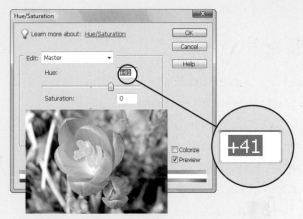

You can create some other great color effects by selecting *Enhance > Adjust Color > **Hue/Saturation***. At its simplest, the *Hue* slider is good for dramatic, artistic effects. Drag this left or right to remap the colors in your image without affecting the brightness and shadow levels.

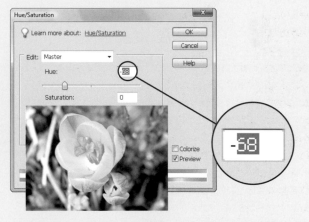

To turn the picture from full-color to a colorized monotone, click the *Colorize* button in this window. Drag the *Hue* slider to change the color, and adjust the *Saturation* to get the right strength. It is good for special graphic effects, but you may prefer to do this to selections *(see pages 92-93)* or layers *(see pages 98-103)* rather than to the whole image.

For more control in the *Hue/Saturation* window, change the pop-up menu at the top from *Master* to a specific color range. Now your changes will affect just one color group rather than everything at once. You can pick the color range you want by using the *Eyedropper* tool and clicking on the color to be altered.

Levels

The *Levels* feature allows you to adjust the tones and color balance of an image by altering the intensity of the image's shadows, midtones, and highlights. While it might look complicated, the *Levels* feature is one of the most powerful tools available in Photoshop Elements and can cure many common image problems.

When you open the *Levels* dialog box, you will see a graph in the center of the window. This represents the tones contained within your image. The left side of the graph displays the amount of shadow tones; in the middle of the graph are the midtones; and on the right of the graph are the highlights. Open different digital photographs and look at their levels to see how the graph works.

▶ PICTURE PERFECT

You can use the *Levels* feature very quickly by selecting *Auto Levels*, accessed via *Enhance > Auto Levels*. This will automatically adjust the color levels of your photograph with surprisingly good results. For greater control, however, it is best to use the *Levels* feature—this allows you to adjust your image manually.

Opening the *Levels* dialog box displays the red, blue, and green channels in your image. At the base of the graph are three markers. These represent the blacks (the shadows), the grays (the midtones), and the whites (the highlights) contained in the image. Moving these markers changes the image's levels. Moving the black marker toward the middle, for example, deepens the shadow areas of your image. Similarly, moving the white marker to the left will brighten highlights.

The *Levels* dialog

As well as correcting the exposure of an image, *Levels* can be used to correct color problems. This photograph of a flowerbed has the wrong white-balance setting.

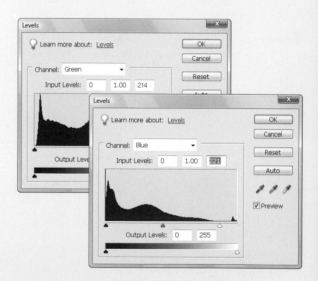

3 The green channel is adjusted to subtly increase its strength. Check the *Preview* box and you will be able to see the effect that your adjustments have on the image.

The blue channel is tweaked in order to remove the blue cast caused by incorrect white balance.

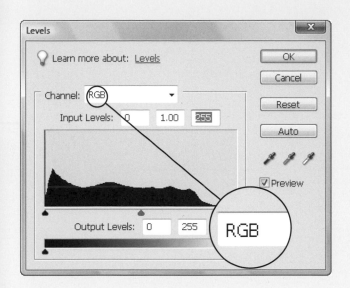

1 The *Levels* dialog box displays the levels of all three channels of the image—the red, green, and blue channels.

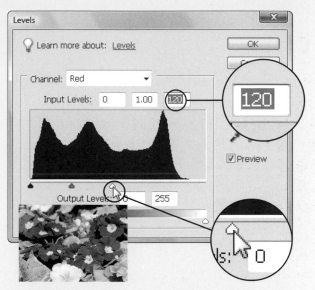

2 Selecting the channels individually in the pop-up menu allows you to change colors in the image independently. Here, the red channel has been adjusted in order to strengthen contrast, deepening the red in the overall image.

The image is adjusted slightly to prevent the reds from appearing too strong.

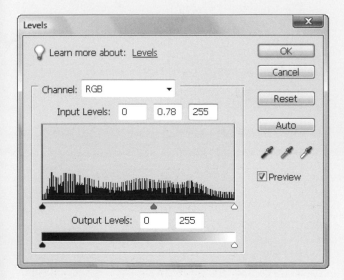

4 As a final finishing touch, fine-tune all three channels at the same time by selecting RGB in the pop-up menu.

5 After a few minutes' work with the *Levels* dialog box, this shot is bursting with deep tones and bright color.

Click!

Layers

Image layers let you stack parts of images together to build up a complete picture. Each layer can be moved about separately and acts like its own self-contained image. If you darken or paint on a layer, other layers will not be affected. Think of a layer as being on its own sheet of glass. You see the layers together, but you can move and work on each one without affecting any of the others. In this way, because you don't have to paint straight onto your photo, you can try things out without messing up the main image.

Each layer can have transparent areas, which makes them useful for collaging pictures. The overall transparency of a layer can also be changed, so you can, for example, make clouds nebulous or turn a person into a ghostlike figure. If you copy and paste something, it will automatically arrive as a new layer. Choose *New* from the *Layer* menu to make an empty layer for painting from scratch. Use the *Move* tool to slide the whole layer to the right place, and the *Layers* palette to choose which layer to work on. Click on the eye icon beside any layer to hide it in the main image.

Watch out for file sizes

Every time you create a new layer, the size of your image is enlarged. An image with too many layers can quickly become too large for your computer to deal with. For this reason, it is best to flatten the image occasionally. The *Flatten Image* option is accessed in the pop-up menu on the *Layers* palette; it reduces file sizes by merging layers in your image. Take care not to flatten the wrong layers when you do this, though.

Using layers

Create new layers by selecting *Layer > New*. *Layer* creates a new blank layer; *Layer From Background* copies the background layer; *Layer via Copy* copies the currently selected layer (or a selection in it); and *Layer via Cut* removes the selection from the old layer and places it in a new one.

The stacking order of layers can be changed to bring one in front of another. Just drag a layer up or down in the *Layers* palette. (The Background layer can't be moved, but if you double-click on that layer, it will be converted to a new, editable layer instead.)

LAYERS

Here, the image of the hand has been brought in front of the leaves in "Layer 2" simply by rearranging the order of the layers.

You may need to "flatten" before you can save an image in certain file formats. This also keeps file sizes down. *Merge Down* merges the selected layer with the one below, while *Merge Visible* flattens all currently visible layers. You can switch their visibility on or off using the eye buttons on the left of the *Layers* palette.

continued on page 100. . .

The *Layers* palette

Working with layers can take a little getting used to, but there are some specific features that will help you get started. First of all, drag the *Layers* palette out of the *Palette Bin* so that it stays open all the time. The *Opacity* slider in the *Layers* palette controls the current layer's transparency. If you want to work on a layer without painting onto transparent areas, click on the small *Lock* button. This "locks" transparent and semitransparent areas, so you can paint in confidence. The *Layer* menu lets you duplicate and delete layers easily, as well as merge layers with others to simplify your *Layers* palette list.

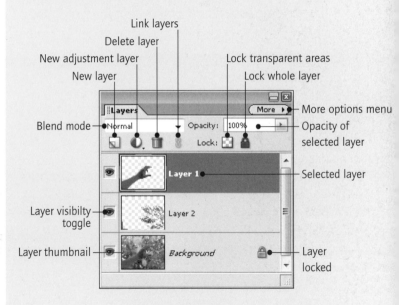

Layers—continued

The best way to understand the benefits of layers is simply to start using them. When you combine layers with the opacity and blend mode controls, you can create any number of exciting effects. Here, we demonstrate how useful layers can be by making a simple layered image using three separate photographs.

▶ **JARGON BUSTER**

Blend modes

As well as allowing you to make composite images from your photographs, layers also offer a wide range of blend modes. With names such as *Dissolve, Multiply, Color Dodge*, and *Hard Light*, blending modes can completely transform an image. Blend modes work by determining how pixels blend with underlying layers in the image. Using the *Difference* blending mode will, for example, have the effect of increasing the contrast of a layer. The *Vivid Light* blending mode, on the other hand, will have the effect of intensifying the layer's color. All of these options are available from the *Blend Mode* menu in the *Layers* palette. Be sure to experiment and learn the effects of the various blending modes.

Combining images with layers

1 Here we have our three shots: two photos of seagulls and a clear blue sky background with a ghostly moon.

4 Now open the first bird image and use the *Magic Wand* tool to select the sky behind the bird. The dotted lines indicate that most of the sky is selected. Choose *Inverse* from the *Select* menu to select the bird itself.

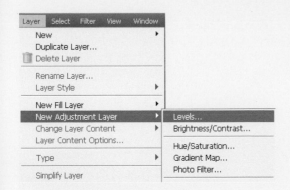

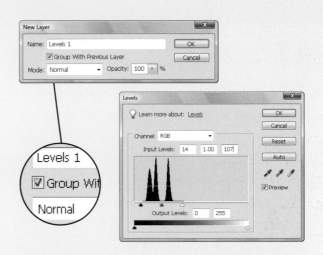

2 We need to brighten up the background sky, using a special type of layer: an adjustment layer. Adjustment layers are transparent layers that seem to alter the tones or colors of layers below, without actually affecting a single pixel. This means that you can continually readjust the adjustment layer without damaging the original image. Select *Layer > New Adjustment Layer > **Levels*** to begin.

3 When the *New Layer* window appears, click on the *Group With Previous Layer* check box. This ensures that the adjustment will affect only the layer directly below it. Move the left slider to the right and the right slider to the left to brighten up the background. Click *OK*.

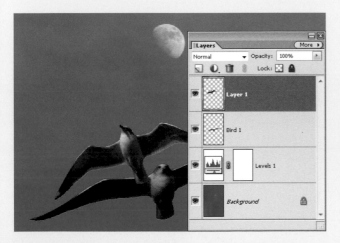

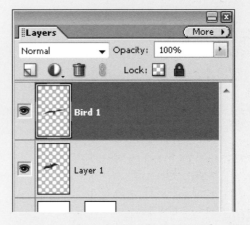

5 Select *Edit > **Copy*** to copy the bird selection, then reopen or select the sky background and choose *Edit > **Paste***. The seagull will be added to the background. Notice that a new layer has been created after pasting in the selection. After pasting in a second bird, there are now two extra layers in the main image.

6 As noted on page 98, by clicking and dragging a layer in the *Layers* palette, it is possible to shift the order of the layers. Here the two bird layers have swapped positions in the layer hierarchy.

continued . . .

LAYERS

101

LAYERS

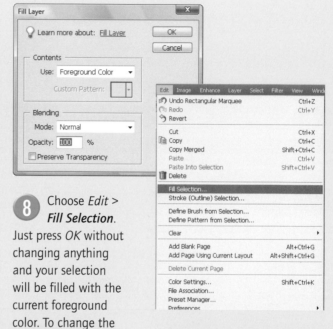

8 Choose *Edit > Fill Selection*. Just press *OK* without changing anything and your selection will be filled with the current foreground color. To change the foreground color, simply click on the colored square at the bottom of the main *Toolbox* and use the *Color Picker*.

7 Let's look at how different layers interact with each other. Select the layer with the second bird in it, then choose *Filter > Blur > **Blur More***. Blur is added to the bird in the background—since this is on its own layer, the rest of the image is unaffected. Now use *Layer > **New Layer*** to create a new layer, then use the *Rectangular Marquee* tool to make a selection on the right of the image.

10 Choosing the *Linear Light* blend will alter the colors in the area below the rectangle, while leaving the bird and sky texture visible.

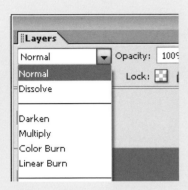

9 The color is added as a layer that sits on top of all the other layers. Clicking on the *Blend Mode* pop-up menu in the *Layers* palette reveals a variety of ways of changing the colored layer.

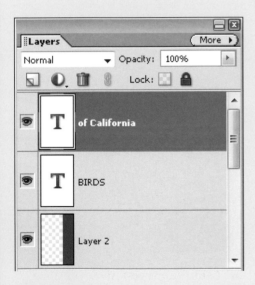

11 Layers can contain any graphic object. Here, text has been added to the picture *(see pages 124-125)*.

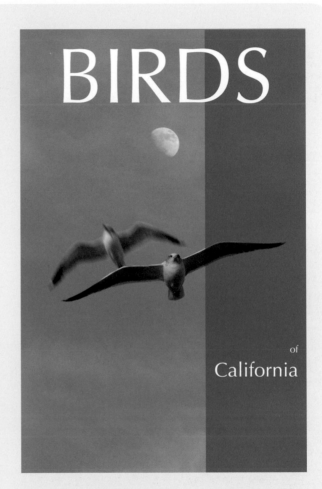

12 Now we can see how the color in the top layer affects the images below it. Notice the change in hue in the gull's wing. Changing the blend mode will change the effect. Try selecting different blend modes from the *Blend Mode* menu and look at the results.

Click!

Changing backgrounds

Layers make it easy to produce composite images made up from many other images. In this example, Adobe Photoshop Elements is used to demonstrate how to separate a subject from its background, using layers to transform the two elements independently.

Most applications have a number of dedicated tools for selecting parts of an image *(see pages 92–93)*. These are known as selection tools, and include the *Marquee* tool, *Lasso* tool and *Magic Wand* tool. The *Marquee* tool allows you to select rectangular or elliptical areas of a picture; the *Lasso* tool allows you to select parts of an image by simply drawing around them; the *Magic Wand* tool allows areas to be selected depending on the color of their pixels.

▶ **PICTURE PERFECT**

Which Lasso?

As we saw earlier, Photoshop Elements has three types of *Lasso*: the *Lasso*, the *Polygonal Lasso,* and the *Magnetic Lasso*. The last is useful when you are trying to select an object that really stands out against its background but is not so useful in other situations. When you don't have enough contrast for the *Magnetic Lasso* to work, use one of the other two *Lassos*. The *Lasso* is fine if you are making broad selections or if you have a steady hand, but try the *Polygonal Lasso* for more detailed work. It makes short work of straight-edged selections, but if you break up curves into a lot of little steps, this tool can be just as effective with curves and irregular shapes.

Separating images

You'll often find yourself wanting to work on parts of an image independently. Once you've made a selection, it is sensible to keep it on a separate layer.

1 Before you start cutting your subject out, think about what selection tools you will use. Here the edges make the *Magnetic Lasso* very tempting, but there are places where the contrast looks low. Instead it would probably be safer to make a *Lasso* selection, then refine it afterward.

3 The separated object is now on its own layer. To see this more clearly, click on the eye logo to the left of the *Background* layer to turn off its visibility.

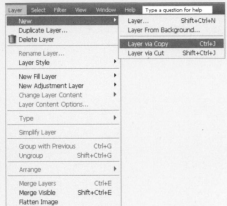

2 Select the standard *Lasso* tool and draw a rough outline of your object. Once a selection marquee has been drawn around the object, you can separate it and place it in its own layer. Use the *Layer via Copy* command in the *Layer* menu.

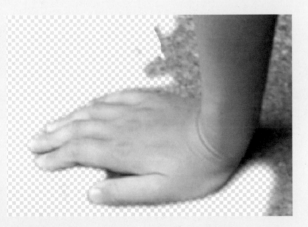

4 Because the cutout is now on a separate layer, you can use the Eraser tool to remove the parts of the image not required. Use the *Tool Options Bar* to change the brush size whenever you need to.

continued on page 106 . . .

The *Magic Wand* tool

The *Magic Wand* tool is excellent for selecting areas of similar color. To use this tool, simply click on a color and the wand will make a selection based on the similarity of surrounding colors. The *Magic Wand* tool is ideal when, for example, you wish to select and isolate an evenly colored blue sky.

Using the *Magnetic Lasso* tool

This example could be approached with the *Magnetic Lasso*. When using the *Magnetic Lasso*, remember to check the *Options Bar* at the top of the screen. The *Width* option adjusts the range around the pointer. Photoshop looks for contrast, and the *Edge Contrast* option sets how strong the edge of the object needs to be for the *Lasso* to follow it. Finally, the *Frequency* sets how often an anchor point (the marks along the line) are placed. The higher the frequency, the more accurate the line, although this can result in a jagged edge.

If you find that a few anchor points have gone astray, you can work backward by pressing the *Backspace* or *Delete* keys. You can also click to add your own anchor points wherever you choose.

Click!

Changing backgrounds—continued

CHANGING BACKGROUNDS

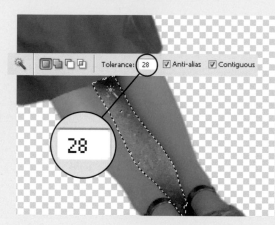

6 To soften the edges with a feather, we must first select our cutout again, as we've changed the edges. The quickest way is to click a transparent area with the *Magic Wand* tool, then invert the selection (*Select > **Inverse***).

5 If you have kept a large area of even color, use the *Magic Wand* tool to select it all at once before deleting. Alter the *Tolerance* amount to adjust how the *Magic Wand* tool picks up surrounding colors. Remember to *Shift-click* if you are adding to an area you've already selected, or *Alt-click* to delete.

8 Create a *Hue/ Saturation* adjustment layer to make the background black and white. Do this by clicking on the background layer, then on the *New Adjustment Layer* button at the bottom of the *Layers* palette. Drag the saturation down to -100 in the resulting dialog box and click *OK*.

9 Duplicate the cutout layer by dragging the layer to the *New Layer* icon at the bottom of the palette. Now drag that copy beneath the *Hue/Saturation* adjustment layer.

10 Apply a strong *Gaussian Blur* to the layer by clicking *Filter > Blur > **Gaussian Blur***.

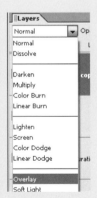

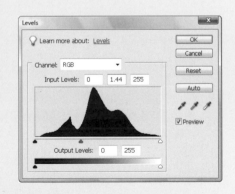

7 Now, before applying your feather, click *Select >*
*Modify > **Contract***. This will bring the selection in
around the girl by one pixel, so the feather we apply has
more effect. Finally apply a feather using *Select > **Feather***.

11 Finally, change the blend mode of the top layer
to *Overlay*. The result has an interesting soft-focus
appearance that also retains much of the sharpness of the
original picture. To finish, apply *Levels* to the background to
make it look slightly different and to make the foreground
stand out even more.

12 The completed image. The neutral background
pushes the foreground out even more.

Building a montage

Making a montage of your favorite pictures is an interesting way of presenting a selection of images from a particular event such as a party or a sightseeing tour. With the level of control that layers and selection tools give you, it is easy to create such a montage using as few or as many images as you like. Here, a trip to Geneva, Switzerland, is captured in a montage that combines snapshots of a young child with an image of the Swiss flag and a bridge over Lake Geneva. As an extra touch, some text has also been added to the image.

▶ PICTURE PERFECT

Hide the joins

One of the biggest challenges when creating a montage is hiding the joins between the images used. Even when you are not trying to create one realistic whole out of three different shots, it can still be offputting if the tones or detail levels in the images don't match. There are two tricks that are often used to disguise any mismatches: you can use the *Blur* or *Noise* filters *(see pages 114–115)* to mask any differences in detail; and you can use the *Levels, Contrast, Color,* and *Exposure* tools to match the colors and tones in the photos as closely as possible. It is better to make the changes before you start the montage, but you can make such adjustments afterward if you need to.

Composition

1 Start with three of your favorite images.

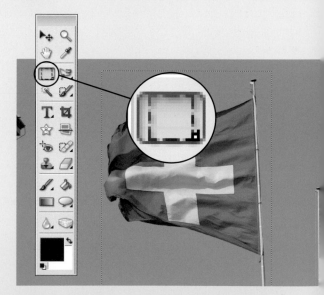

4 Next, the *Marquee* tool is used to select the part of the Swiss flag image that will be retained. Because the background on this layer does not need such careful selection, a large box is drawn around it.

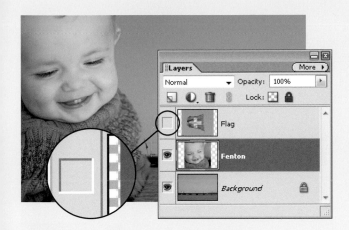

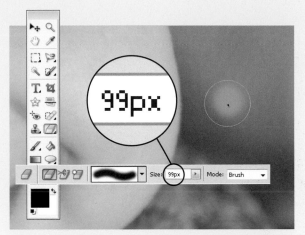

2 Begin by adding all of your images to the main picture. Here the picture of a bridge taken in Geneva is used as the background. The images of the child and the Swiss flag are then added.

The layer containing the Swiss flag is turned off by clicking the *Eye* icon in the *Layers* palette. This makes it easier to work on the layer containing the child, which is rotated and placed on the left of the image.

3 The *Eraser* tool is used to remove the background from the picture of a child. Choose a large, soft-edged brush from the brush drop-down menu, and set the size to 99 pixels. Take your time here; you can use your mouse to remove large chunks away from the child's face, but use many smaller strokes when you are working next to the skin.

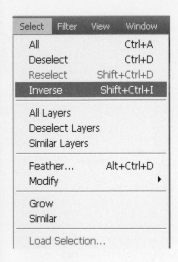

5 The box is then inverted so that everything in the image, except the original box, is selected.

6 The inverted part of the image is deleted *(Edit > Delete)*, leaving just the flag and a small amount of sky remaining.

continued . . .

Building a montage—continued

7 The images are now ready to be moved and manipulated to complete the final effect.

8 A blend mode *(see page 100)* of *Linear Light* is first used to give the flag more graphic impact.

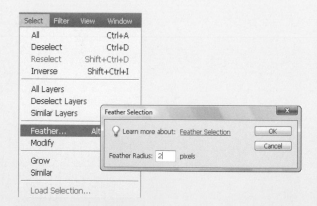

11 Next, the edges of the selection are feathered—this is to prevent the selection from looking too clumsy and severe. The *Feather* setting that you use depends on the size of the original image—high-resolution images usually require a higher *Feather* setting.

12 Feathering a selection will often leave a small border around the selection. This can easily be erased using a small *Eraser* brush. Set the size to 10 pixels or less.

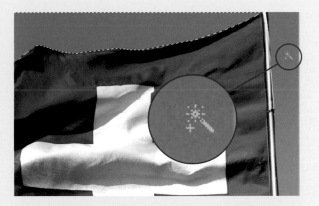

9 Next, the *Magic Wand* tool is used to select the sky surrounding the flag so that it can be removed. The *Magic Wand* tool has a *Tolerance* setting that controls its ability to select colors. Lower the *Tolerance* setting if you select too much of the image; increase the *Tolerance* setting if too little of the image is selected.

10 Clicking on the blue sky area of the flag layer will select most of the sky. Holding down the *Shift* key and clicking again allows you to add more to the selection.

13 To improve the composition of the image, the flagpole was extended using the *Clone* tool.
Alt-clicking on the flagpole creates a selection point for the *Clone* tool. Painting carefully beneath the flagpole will extend it.

14 The final image. Adding text to the picture creates a nice finishing touch. Here, *Glow* has been applied to the text to make it stand out from the background. *(See pages 124-125 for more on adding text.)*

Masks

Masks are an important feature of digital photography and are present in most image-editing software packages. Masks do exactly as their name suggests—they are used to mask out parts of an image. Masks are similar in function to using masking tape to prevent paint from being accidentally splashed onto the glass when painting around a window. A digital mask masks out part of an image from the effect you are applying. Masks are particularly useful when you are working with color corrections, cloning, and levels.

When you paint a mask, you make a selection of everything outside the mask. Using the *Invert Selection* command, you can use a selection as a mask or a mask as a selection—the choice is yours. In this example, we look at ways of masking out parts of an image so that the exposure can be adjusted in specific sections of an image. This is a very simple technique—especially in applications such as Adobe Photoshop Elements, which has a dedicated *Mask Brush* tool. Using masks will enable you to have greater control over the way you create your finished, retouched images.

Using the *Selection Brush* tool

1 This image has great potential but was taken without a flash, making the face appear too dark. This oversight can be fixed by altering the levels of the face. A mask is required to ensure that levels on other parts of the picture are not changed.

Select the *Selection Brush* tool. This allows you to paint a mask onto your picture.

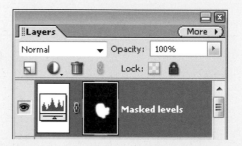

4 Create a *Levels Adjustment Layer* to alter the tones of the image. (If you want to link it to the layer beneath, click *Layer > Group With Previous*.)

Either way, something interesting has occurred in the *Layers* palette. To the right of the *Levels* icon is a strange-looking black and white object—this is the mask you have just created. The white-colored area indicates where the adjustment is taking place; the area in black remains unaffected by the adjustment.

2 Check that the mode is set to mask in the *Options Bar*. You can then click and drag the mouse over the subject's face and a red "paint" will appear.

3 When completed, invert the mask selection by using the *Inverse* command from the *Select* menu.

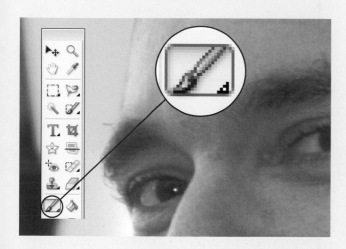

5 Layer masks can be retouched. Click on the layer mask to select it, then select the standard *Brush* tool and paint onto the main picture. Painting with black will increase the mask, while painting with white will remove it. A little black has been painted around the edge of the mask to help it adhere to the contours of the face more accurately.

6 With the mask in place, *Levels* was used to correct the underexposure in the face without affecting the tones of the background.

INTRODUCING FILTERS

Introducing filters

Filters are the special-effects tools of Photoshop Elements and are among the most gratifying things you can use in this program. They can change your photos in many ways, ranging from the standard sharpening and blurring features through to the wilder effects of *Find Edges* and *Zig Zag*. Many of these effects simulate different forms of artistic media, from paint effects such as *Palette Knife, Rough Pastels,* and *Watercolor* to more extreme media such as *Stained Glass* and *Mosaic*. It is well worth playing with filters for a while. They can be very flexible and tend to behave a little differently with every image.

Applying filters to images is simply a matter of picking one from the *Filter* menu, or browsing through the list in the *Filters* section of the *Artwork and Effects* palette (under *Special Effects*) and clicking the Apply button. Some filters work immediately, others have a set of controls and will open either an individual dialog box, or within the *Filter Gallery,* where you can adjust their settings, and, in many instances, preview the effect to help you decide whether or not to use it. To see which filters have customization options, find them in the Filter menu: if their names end with three dots (*Add Noise...*, for example) they will have custom settings available.

Using filters and the *Filters* palette

Applying a filter to a whole image may sometimes be too heavy-handed. If you'd like to use a filter on just part of an image instead, the techniques covered in Selections *(see pages 92–93)* and in Layers *(see pages 98–103)* can prove extremely useful. Applying filters to just a part of your image, using feathered selection edges or layer transparency to blend things if you want, will yield more subtle results. If you duplicate a layer before applying a filter, then reducing the transparency of the filtered layer tones down the effect.

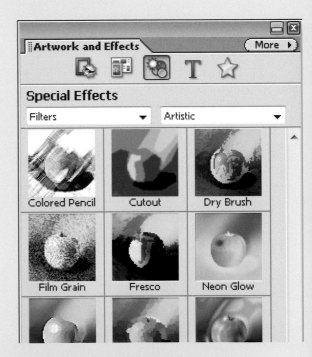

The *Filters* section of the *Artwork and Effects* palette shows a small thumbnail example of the effects of each filter. You can pick specific categories of filters using the menu at the top-right of the window. To use a filter, you can either double-click the icon, or single-click to select it and press the Apply button.

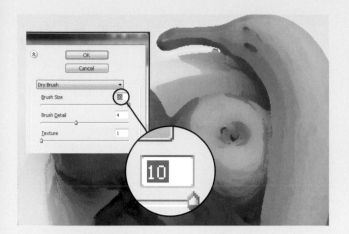

The *Dry Brush* filter

The *Dry Brush* filter can be very effective at simulating the look of a watercolor or oil brush on dry paper without going over the top. As with most filter controls, the standard settings are generally pretty good, but try different settings for the brush size and detail, and a lower texture setting, too.

The *Liquify* filter

Liquify is one of the most dramatic filters on offer. It lets you push the image around as if it were, well, liquid. Different effects include *Turbulence*, *Twirl*, *Bloat*, and *Reflection*. There's also a very useful *Reconstruct* tool for restoring a distorted area to its original state.

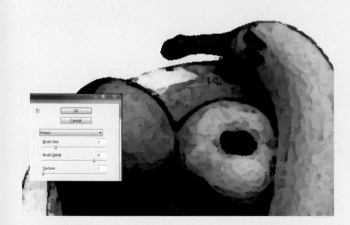

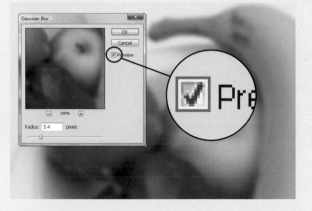

The *Fresco* filter

More dramatic effects can be made with filters such as *Fresco,* which recreates the image using short, rounded dabs of color applied in an almost frenzied manner. As with *Dry Brush*, use the controls to change the size and detail of the brush and the surface texture amount.

The *Blur* filters

Gaussian Blur is the most useful blur filter, since it lets you pick just how much blurring to apply. The *Radius* amount sets how wide the blur should be—the effect can be seen in the small sample box above. If the *Preview* box is checked too, the whole image changes.

Creating a work of art

Combining masks with layers and filters gives you complete creative control over your photographs. As well as being able to create montages and alter specific areas of an image, you can also use these features to create works of art. This is the point when digital photography comes into its own—effects that would once have been possible only by using expensive design equipment can now be created using a home computer and the relevant image-editing software.

This next exercise demonstrates how effects can be used to totally transform the appearance of an image. In this way, photographs can be made to look as if they were painted in watercolor, oil, or any other artistic medium. The techniques outlined here can be adapted to work with many different types of digital photographs. For example, here we are strengthening the colors, but you may wish to reduce them for a washed-out feel.

As always, remember to make a copy of your original photograph first. This will allow you to experiment with the image without the risk of losing the original forever.

Unleash the artist inside you

Using the tools available in Adobe Photoshop Elements, it is possible to transform any photograph into a work of art. The bright colors in this shot of a park in Switzerland make it an ideal image to work with.

1 Open the original image in Adobe Photoshop Elements.

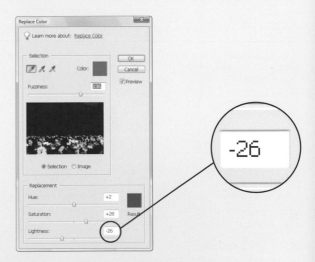

4 The same technique is again used to change the image's blues and purples.

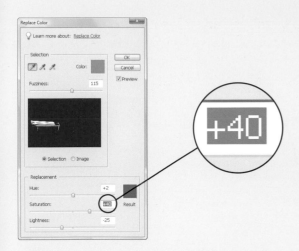

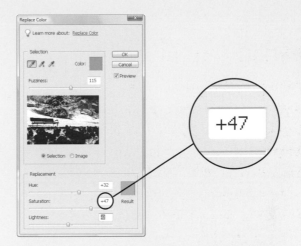

2 Begin by adding some strong colors into the picture. Select the *Replace Color* enhancement tool. Clicking on the red chair selects its colors, and adjusting the *Fuzziness* level widens the range of similar colors in the image. Once the colors are selected, use *Hue/Saturation* and *Brightness* to change their levels. Here the *Saturation* of the reds has been increased, making them richer and deeper.

3 After applying the *Replace Color* command for the red chair, it is again used to select the greens in the image to increase their strength.

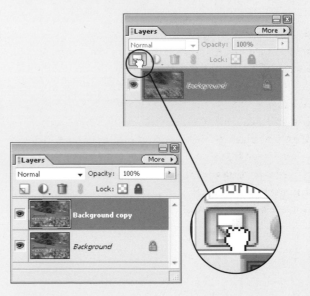

5 The image now has strong, hyper-real reds, greens, and blues, giving the photo a feel of electronic art (or at least a badly adjusted TV screen).

6 At the moment this is only one layer in the image. Dragging the layer down to the central *Duplicate Layer* icon at the bottom of the *Layers* palette will create a copy of the image on a new layer.

continued . . .

Creating a work of art—continued

7 With the new layer selected, choose the *Water Paper* filter from the *Filter* menu. This has a number of options to experiment with. Start with subtle settings, then nudge the sliders right, according to taste.

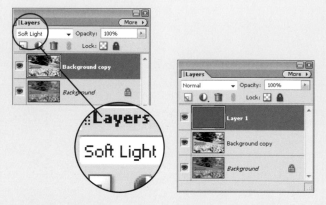

8 Next, apply a blending mode of *Soft Light* to the layer. This will add some of the look of the new layer to the original. Now create a new blank layer and fill it with a mid-gray color using the *Paint Bucket* tool.

11 Finally, create a painted appearance at the edges of the image with a paintbrush. Before painting, increase the canvas size of the image. Ensure that the background color in the *Tool* palette is set to white.

12 There are dozens of paintbrush options in Adobe Photoshop Elements that can be used to create different styles of painting. Here, a *Charcoal* brush has been selected in the *Natural Brushes* set.

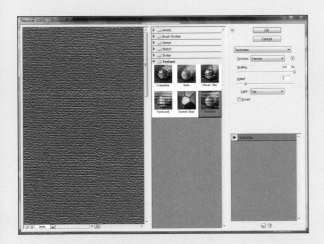

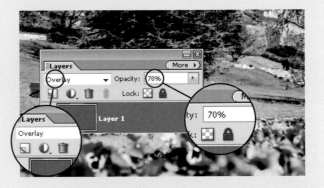

9 Now select the *Texturizer* filter from the main menu. The *Texturizer* allows many different types of texture to be applied to a layer.

10 The gray, textured layer has been positioned above the main image. The layer's blending mode has been changed to *Overlay* to apply the "look" of the textured layer without the gray color. For subtlety, the layer's *Opacity* has been reduced to 70%.

13 With white selected as the foreground color, the border is painted in a random manner.

14 Why not add your signature to your masterpiece? For this sort of task you might want to buy a graphics tablet. It can be attached to your computer and allows you to draw with a pressure-sensitive "pen" into programs like Photoshop Elements.

Panoramas

The wide-angle setting of your lens works well for many different types of pictures, but sometimes it is simply not wide enough. There is, however, a solution to this problem, which is known as panorama photography. Panoramas work by combining a number of photographs taken at the same location to produce a single seamless image. This process can be a very difficult task to achieve manually. Fortunately, image-editing programs such as Adobe Photoshop Elements allow you to create panoramas automatically.

In traditional film photography, the type of picture shown opposite was almost impossible to create accurately. With the correct software, however, panoramas can be relatively straightforward to produce digitally. Photomerge, Photoshop Elements' built-in option, automatically creates panoramas.

To prepare a series of images for use in Photomerge, you should ideally use a tripod. Find a location that gives you an unrestricted view of your setting. Set up the tripod and ensure that the camera is level. If your camera allows it, set its exposure manually. Evaluate the exposure using the camera's automatic setting and then set the manual exposure to the same. This will give you an even exposure on each frame.

To prepare photographs correctly for Photomerge, each of the shots that you take needs to overlap slightly. Choose a starting point for your pa norama and turn the camera in a clockwise direction on your tripod as you take each successive photograph. Use easily recognizable objects as reference points. If the first shot contains a tree in the right of the shot, for example, make sure the next shot has that same tree in the left of the frame. Continue taking shots and using reference points in the pictures until you have covered your whole subject. You are then ready to use Photomerge.

Using Photomerge

1 Save all the images that you wish to merge into one folder on your computer.

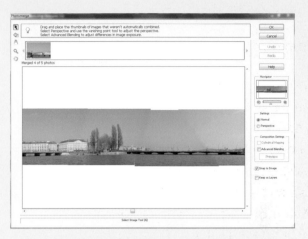

2 Select *New > **Photomerge Panorama*** from the *File* menu. Use the Photomerge browser to locate the files you want to merge into a panorama.

3 Photomerge works automatically to stitch all of the images together. Sometimes, however, images need individual adjustment.

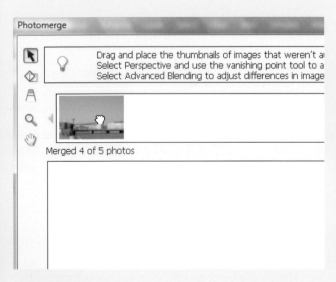

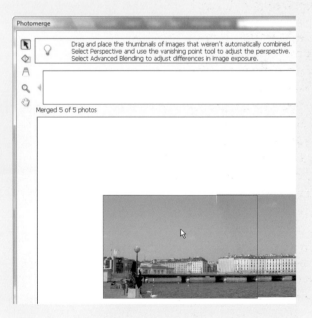

4 Here, Photomerge's misreading of the edges of the images is corrected using the *Hand* tool to move the overall image to the left.

5 The image from the bar at the top of the screen is dragged and dropped onto the main image. As this happens, the two images merge slightly.

continued . . .

Panoramas—continued

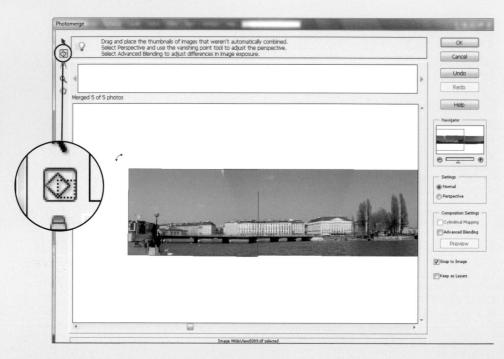

6 Because this panorama was created without the use of a tripod, there is a degree of inaccuracy in the straightness of the horizon. Use the Photomerge *Rotate* tool to fine-tune the image.

As you can see from the picture above, the tool has now merged all five of the source images into a long strip. Hit *OK* or *Enter*, and Photomerge will perform the calculations necessary to create the panorama.

7 Use the *Clone* tool to do a little additional cleaning. Zoom into the areas where the images join and correct any major flaws in the panorama.

8 Finally, use the *Crop* tool to select the area of the image you wish to keep. If necessary, rotate the crop in order to straighten the horizon.

Adding text to images

Text can be added to an image in all sorts of interesting ways. Text can provide extra information or bring humor to an image; it can turn your picture into a greeting card or postcard that can be printed, emailed, or presented on your website. Graphic designers spend a lot of time ensuring that the text they select fits in well with an image. This is an art in itself but you, too, can achieve good results adding text in your photographs simply by following a few easy rules.

Most home computers have a wide range of fonts already installed. Resist the temptation to use too many of these in a single image. In general, it is preferable to use only one font, or possibly two that complement one another. Before you add text to an image, think about the picture and the message you intend to convey. Is it a serious message such as a Get Well greeting? Or is it a humorous message that belongs on a birthday card? The photograph and the font that you use should reinforce and enhance your message.

▶ JARGON BUSTER

Serif and sans serif

Serif   Sans serif

There are two basic types of fonts—serif and sans serif. Fonts such as Times and Courier are both serif fonts—that is, they have additional decoration at the end of each line of each character. Sans serif fonts, such as Arial, have no such decoration.

The *Text* tool

1 Begin by selecting the *Text* tool in the *Tool* palette. Selecting the *Text* tool reveals a number of options that can alter the appearance of your text. Here, it is possible to control the type of font, its alignment, and even make the text follow a curve.

The point size of the text is selected. As soon as you click on the image and begin typing, the text will appear in its own layer.

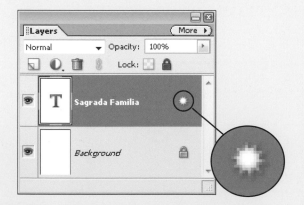

4 The text sits in its own layer in the *Layers* palette. The white starburst icon indicates when you have added a layer effect to the layer.

2 You can use the *Move* tool to fine-tune the position of your text.

The text is now an object on the layer that can be freely moved. It is even possible to reduce or increase the size of the text if the size you selected is incorrect.

3 Adobe Photoshop Elements has a wide range of layer styles available for adding effects to a text layer. Here, the *Drop Shadow* options are used to place a small shadow effect behind the text.

You can also add a *Bevel* effect, which will give the text a slightly three-dimensional appearance.

5 Double-clicking the starburst icon enables you to customize any effect you have applied to the text. Here, the direction of the light and its accompanying shadow can be changed, as well as the strength of the shadow.

Scanning

On occasion you may need to make a digital version of an old photograph. It may be that you wish to create extra copies of an old print print it out at a larger size, or manipulate the photograph with image-editing software. To do this, you will need a scanner. This piece of equipment works by reading—or scanning—all of the information in an image and converting that information into digital information.

▶ JARGON BUSTER

Types of scanners

There are many different scanners available, ranging in price and quality from machines that cost less than a hundred dollars through to professional models that cost many thousands of dollars. Before you decide which scanner to purchase, it is wise to think about the types of images you intend to scan, and what you wish to do with those scanned images. There are two main types of scanners available: flatbed scanners allow you to scan flat objects including photographs, books, and magazines, plus any other object that can fit under the lid. Film scanners scan film negatives and slides at higher resolutions than a flatbed scanner can manage. However, transparency adapters are available that allow a flatbed scanner to do a similar job with very acceptable levels of quality.

Scanning know-how

Scanning in traditional photographs allows you to manipulate them in an image-editing program such as Adobe Photoshop Elements. With such a digital bag of tricks, you can bring new life to old photographs.

Many different types of objects can be scanned on a flatbed scanner. This CD was an easy element to scan because it is flat. There are a variety of uses for a scan such as this. Here the CD scan has been cut out, duplicated onto three layers, distorted, blurred, and pasted into a colorful background.

This Color!

It is often useful to be able to scan objects to use in illustrations. Here, a piece of colorful cloth has been scanned in. The addition of some text enables you to specify the color of the cloth and then email the image to a friend.

When scanning objects that might scratch the scanner's surface, protect the scanner by placing a sheet of transparent plastic on the glass.

continued on page 128 . . .

Scanners: a buyer's guide

When choosing a scanner, there are a few things you should look out for:

• The most important is the optical resolution, which is the maximum number of pixels the scanner can capture, measured in dots per inch (dpi). Generally speaking, the higher the better, but remember that most home printers cannot make use of anything higher than 300 dpi, so unless you intend to scale up your images, a 300 dpi resolution will be acceptable.

• Be wary of the widely used, but essentially meaningless, "interpolated resolution" that many scanners quote. This is simply image information guessed at by the computer if you go above the scanner's optical resolution. If a scanner offers a resolution of 9,600 dpi, don't be fooled.

• The color depth is another significant factor. This is usually measured in bits per pixel. The "bits" in question are the units of information that the computer uses to store color descriptions. Again, higher means better. For Photoshop Elements, and most other software, 24-bit (which translates as 16.8 million colors) is the maximum color depth you will use. If you have Photoshop, it can handle 48-bit color, so it is worth getting a higher color depth scanner to match.

• Naturally, you need to check the size of the scanning area. A Letter (A4)-size flatbed scanner will still get good results for smaller images, but anything larger tends to be too specialized and expensive.

• Finally, some scanners come with sheet feeders that can handle batches—great if you want to archive your old snaps on the computer. Others have film reader attachments. If you are likely to need this feature, ensure such an adapter is available for your scanner.

Click!

Scanning—continued

Scanners usually come with their own scanning software. Depending on the manufacturer, such software varies in quality and ease of use. Some scanners come "bundled" with software that allows you to undertake basic editing (that is, the software is included free). Others provide plug-ins that allow you to scan straight into image-editing packages such as Adobe Photoshop Elements. Unfortunately for the consumer, no two scanner software packages are the same.

Although different brands of scanners have different controls and scanning software, scanners usually operate in pretty much the same way. Most scanners, for example, offer a preview mode. This is a low-resolution scan that allows you to preview and fine-tune your image prior to scanning at a higher resolution. Because scanning at high resolution takes longer to do, this is a welcome feature and can save you a lot of time.

Scanner controls

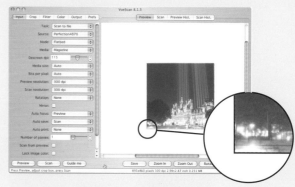

This screenshot is taken from software that was bundled with a Hewlett Packard flatbed scanner. Here, a photograph has been scanned for preview. Previews allow you to make adjustments to images before scanning at a higher resolution. Instead of selecting the whole area of the scanner, only the area containing the print is selected.

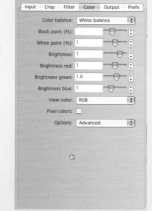

Different scanner software offers different ways of correcting color. What you see here is a typical interface. It is here that the image can be color-corrected. By moving the sliders to cancel the color cast, you can correct the image before scanning it at a higher resolution.

SCANNING

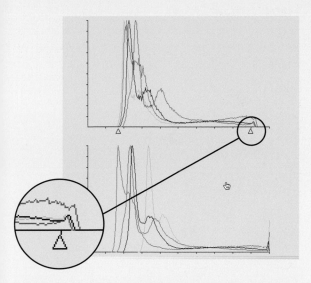

Most scanner software will offer some control of levels and curves. Here, a *Histogram Adjustment* tool is used to brighten the image's highlights.

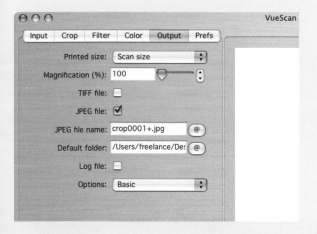

This scanner software allows the file to be saved in several different formats, including JPEG and TIFF. Many scanners, such as the Hewlett Packard one used here, come equipped with a suite of software that allows you to use your scanner creatively.

Fine-tuning your scans

The fine-tuning tools available as part of most scanner software often resemble the color, curves, and levels controls that are standard features in most image-editing software. These tools allow you to inspect the exposure and color balance of your scan and correct it at the preview stage. A crop tool is usually available, allowing you to control the size of area to be scanned.

One final control available for use at the preview stage is the resolution setting. With this setting it is possible to specify the size and resolution of the image. This is very important if you intend to output your image to an inkjet or laser printer. A scan of 300 dpi or higher will usually yield high-quality results.

While your scanner has a certain optical resolution, you need not keep the image the same size in your computer. Many scanners will allow you to scan at 600 dpi, for example, and yet save the file as 300 dpi. This has the effect of doubling the size of the image. This works because the resolution information that the computer stores is simply a little note at the beginning of the file to tell it how large it should be. All your scanner software is doing is allowing you to fool that system. You can do the same thing in Photoshop by clicking *Image > Resize > Image Size...*, then unchecking the *Resample Image* box at the bottom of the dialog box.

Click!

Salvage and repair

One of the most interesting aspects of owning a scanner is that it enables you to scan in old or damaged photographs and use image-editing software to help return them to their former glory. Even if you don't have a scanner, there are still ways of transferring your treasured photographs onto your computer by using just your digital camera.

SALVAGE AND REPAIR

Using the macro setting of your camera, take close-up images of your photos, making sure that the photograph and the camera are perfectly aligned. Fix the photograph against a vertical surface and balance the camera on a book or a tripod if you have one. Ensure that the lighting is as bright and even as possible. Finally, check your digital picture for any reflections of hard lights—adjusting the lighting now makes your job easier at the digital retouching stage.

Open your scanned photograph in an image-editing program and plan the repairs that need to be made. Over the years the photograph may have picked up tears, scratches, and creases, for example. Some types of damage can be very challenging—if, for instance, portions of your image are missing, it will take time and patience to repair.

▶ PICTURE PERFECT

Blemishes first, corrections last

Always repair the scratches and blemishes in your photograph before changing the tone, exposure, sharpness, or contrast. When you make such changes, their calculations are based on every pixel in the image and so, with a damaged image, it is best to make sure the damage does not affect the calculations.

Fixing rips and tears

When restoring, no two images are ever quite the same. Remember the weapons in your armory—especially cloning and copying—as you look at the picture and plan your fixes.

1 This picture, probably taken back in the 1950s, is clearly in need of repair.

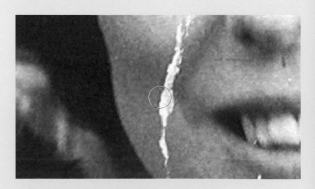

4 As long as the correct source point is selected, it is relatively easy to clone skin tones and remove the scratches.

2 The first step is to identify what repairs need to be made. Note that there are several key areas here that need to be fixed. Particularly challenging is the crease down the middle of the photograph that has removed the surface of the paper.

3 Using the *Clone* tool, it is easy to remove some of the surface marks. Successful cloning depends on the angle at which you sample the image. Sampling along the line between the bricks, by holding *Alt* as you click on them, is the best choice here. Resample *(Alt-click)* often and in different places to avoid creating repeating patterns.

5 The area of the eye is probably the hardest part to tackle. This problem calls for using a different technique to repair the damage.

Select the *Marquee* tool and make a selection around the undamaged eye, then feather (*Select > **Feather**...*) the edge of the selection to give it a soft edge.

6 Create a new layer—this is where a copy of the good eye will be placed.

Use the *Move* tool to move the copy of the eye over to the other side of the face. Place it near, but not over, the damaged part of the image.

Make sure that you have the correct layer selected before you start moving the eye.

continued . . .

Click!

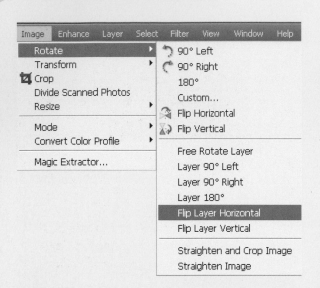

8 Use the *Free Transform* tool to rotate the undamaged eye so that it closely resembles the damaged part of the picture.

7 Now flip the eye horizontally so that it looks as if it belongs on the left side of the face.

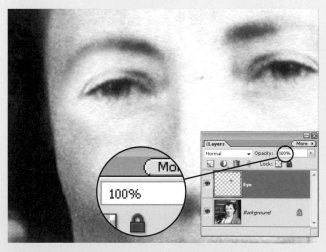

11 Position the new eye over the old one—note that you can still see the tear showing through.

12 Once the eye is in place, turn the opacity of the layer back up to 100%. Because only a small part of the eye needed to be repaired, it is possible to erase most of this new layer. Gently use the *Erase* tool to do this.

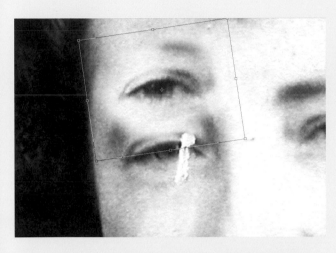

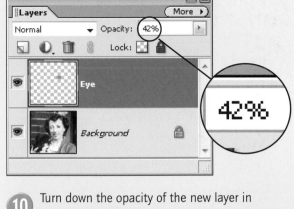

9 Here you can see the undamaged eye after being flipped and placed close to the damaged eye.

10 Turn down the opacity of the new layer in the *Layers* palette—this makes the new layer semitransparent, so that it can be aligned to the background layer easily.

13 The repair is complete, and successful. The retouching work is almost unnoticeable.

14 As a finishing touch, a sepia-tone effect was added to the image. Learn how to create similar sepia-tone effects on pages 134–137.

Sepia and vignette

Adding a sepia-tone effect can add atmosphere or give an old-fashioned appeal to a photograph. The following example demonstrates how to create a sepia-toned picture and mask it using a technique known as a vignette—this will add a soft edge to your picture.

All the tools needed for this simple task are available within Adobe Photoshop Elements as well as other image-editing software packages. Here, we've used a picture taken in Dubai by photographer Graham Cooper as our example.

▶ PICTURE PERFECT

Less is more
When applying effects to your images, think about how appropriate they are. Unless you are aiming for humorous results, a sepia tone will look strange when your subject is a modern skyline or someone wearing modern clothing. Use effects only when they enhance your picture.

Aging a photograph

1 Open your image. Before you do anything else, double-click on the background layer to unlock it. You might want to rename the layer "Picture" in the *New Layer* dialog box that appears. This will keep things clear later on.

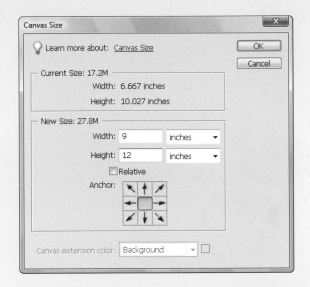

2 Select *Layer > New > **Layer...*** to create a blank layer called "Vignette," then repeat to create a second blank layer called "Background." Move the "Background" layer beneath the "Picture" layer.

3 You will need more space for the vignette, so select *Image > Resize > **Canvas Size*** and add about 2 inches (5 cm) to the numbers in the *Width* and *Height* boxes. This has the effect of adding 1 inch (2.5 cm) all the way around the image.

4 Select the "Background" layer created earlier and choose *Edit > **Fill Layer*** to fill it with white (selected from the top pull-down menu).

5 You can see the white "Background" layer behind the image, occupying the new space created by resizing the canvas.

continued . . .

Sepia and vignette—continued

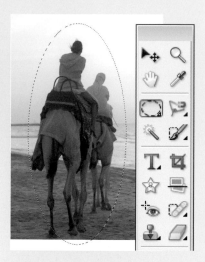

6 Select the "Picture" layer and pick the *Elliptical Marquee* tool. Click above the head of the rider and drag the marquee down and over the camel.

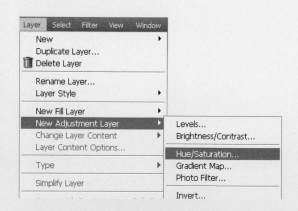

9 Now for the sepia effect. First, go to the *Layer* menu and create a new *Hue/Saturation* adjustment layer.

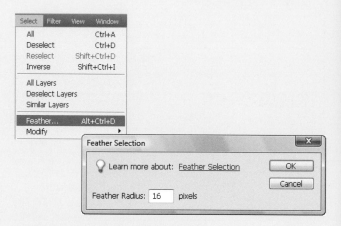

7 Choose *Select > Feather* and add a *Feather Radius* of 16 pixels to the selection. This creates the soft edge required for the vignette effect.

10 Select the option *Group With Previous Layer*, then click *OK*. In the dialog box, click *Colorize*, then change the *Hue* to 31 and the *Saturation* to 17. Click *OK*.

SEPIA AND VIGNETTE

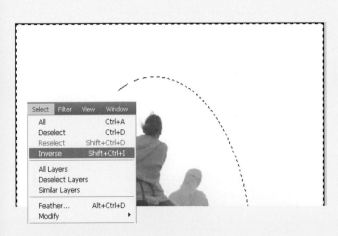

Now choose *Select* > **Inverse** to invert the selection, and then press the *Delete* key. The rest of the layer will now disappear, leaving only the vignette.

The tones will now need some work. Create a new *Levels* adjustment layer, group that layer with the *Picture* layer, and adjust the *Levels* to taste.

To finish, select the background layer and use *Hue/Saturation* to change the color. Here, salmon pink was selected for an attractive period feel.

Storage

Digital photographs are far more resistant to damage than traditional photographs. Digital photographs cannot be creased, torn, or dropped into puddles of water. Nor will they scratch or pick up dust. Digital photographs are not, however, indestructible—a calamitous computer-system crash can rob you of thousands of your valuable images; for this reason it is always sensible to keep a backup of your photographs.

The simplest means of ensuring the safe storage of your images is to make copies of them. Writable CDs or DVDs are a very easy and affordable option for making backups of your image collections. Most recent PCs and Apple Macintosh computers come equipped with built-in CD burners. For those without this feature, however, an external CD burner is an excellent investment.

The latest Apple Macintosh computers boast a SuperDrive—a drive that can burn both CDs and DVDs. While CDs are capable of storing large quantities of your images, a DVD can store much more. Standard CDs are capable of storing approximately 650Mb of data; DVDs, however, can hold up to 4700Mb or 4.7Gb of data—this means literally thousands of digital images.

Adobe Photoshop Elements Organizer

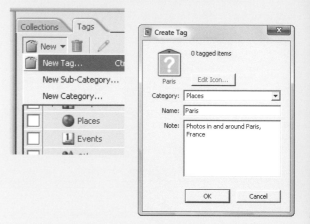

Organizer is a storage and archiving tool for all your digital images. When used alongside Elements itself, Organizer provides a powerful means of both managing and editing your digital photograph libraries.

Organizer enables you to add keywords—or tags—to your images. You are able to define these tags yourself, then search for them.

Once you have created a tag, it is displayed in the *Tags* window. Now all you need to do is drag and drop a tag onto an image or group of images.

Here a number of images have been labeled with the Paris tag.

Apple iPhoto

Apple's free iPhoto software is ideal for storing, sorting, and sharing your photographs.

iPhoto comes equipped with a burn function. This allows you to select albums of photographs and burn them safely onto CD or DVD.

iPhoto also allows you to create keywords and attach them to images. This will enable you to find images quickly, even when your library begins to grow.

This screen shot shows images being searched for and selected by keyword. The keywords feature allows you to have as many keywords as you want.

iPhoto enables you to create a range of professional-looking picture albums that can be printed at home or at a print store.

Cataloging your images

Cataloging your images is very important. To facilitate this task, applications such as Apple iPhoto and Elements Organizer can become indispensable. With these programs it is possible to view all of your photographs in a simple browser, to add keywords to your photographs so that you can search for them later, and to automatically create CD or DVD archives of your images. You can even browse on your computer for images that are stored off-line or on a CD or DVD. This means that you can search your entire digital photograph library for images, without having to keep them all stored on your computer.

Printing, showing, and sharing

What's the point of taking great pictures if you can't show them off? Here we explore how to ensure that you end up with the highest-quality prints. And you don't need to settle for just prints. Why not have some fun and try your hand at using your photos to make personalized bookmarks, or frame your prints with fancy backgrounds? Better still, why not put your pictures on the Web, or surprise friends and family with a pictorial email?

Home printing

Digital photography has another great advantage over traditional film photography—it allows you to create your own prints without messy chemicals or the need to set up a darkroom. Within minutes, digital photographers can have crisp, high-quality prints. All that is needed to make this possible is a home computer and an inexpensive inkjet printer. The box on the right contains some general printing know-how for you to read before you start.

▶ **PICTURE PERFECT**

Types of prints

Many photo-processing facilities offer printing services for digital photographers—you simply take in your digital memory cards and they will output high-quality prints or transfer your images onto a CD. You may even find that in some instances it is less expensive to use a photo-processing facility than to print your own photos. Printing photographs on your home printer, however, does offer a number of advantages and gives you far greater control. As well as using standard photo paper, for example, you can print out your images on a variety of different media, including T-shirts, stickers, cards, and CD covers.

iPhoto

Using Apple's free image-editing program iPhoto, it is possible to create your own stylish photo album. If you have your own printer, this type of project can be fun and is very practical for showcasing your photos.

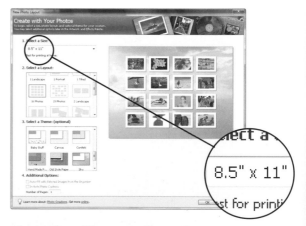

Photoshop Elements Organizer

Using Windows and Photoshop Elements Organizer, you can automatically create projects to print using wizards—step-by-step routines that help with common tasks. Here, a wizard is being used to create a themed multi-photo layout.

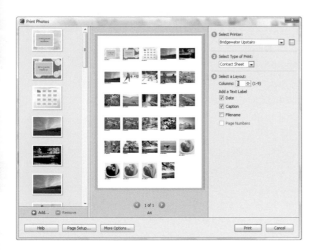

Printing options

Before you print, check the options available. In some programs, including Photoshop Elements, it is possible to create "contact sheets" with multiple images per page to help you catalog your shots.

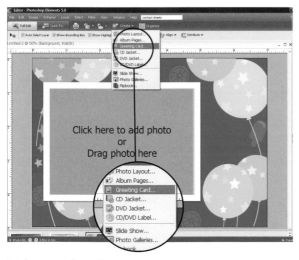

Using a wizard

There are many different types of wizards available in Elements Organizer. This wizard, for example, can be used to make a greeting card.

How an inkjet printer works

Inkjet printers are the most affordable type of printer on the market. They work by spraying minute droplets of ink onto the paper. Although slow, this process can produce results that rival professional prints. Inkjets work best if you print out your images on special paper. These thick, glossy photo papers hold the ink in place, while their reflective surfaces make the colors look brighter. You will get the best results by using the paper recommended by the printer's manufacturer, since on less expensive papers the ink tends to spread, making the image look less sharp.

Other types of color printers

You may also come across a few other types of printer, though none really has the universal flexibility of the home inkjet. Most common are laser printers, which you may have seen in your office at work. Using similar technology to photocopiers, they are fast and ideally suited to a heavy workload, but color machines are expensive, especially those of good quality. You might also come across dye-sublimation printers, which produce very accurate colors and are often used to proof work by designers. The wax cartridges they use make them very expensive to operate.

Buying an inkjet printer

For home use, the inkjet has quickly become the standard because of its quality, flexibility, and ease of use. Because of the vast range of different brands and models available, however, it is important to consider a number of factors before making your selection.

Hidden costs

The main expense of inkjet printing is not the printer itself, but the ink cartridges that you need to keep it running. If you want to keep costs low, avoid printers that use a single ink cartridge for both black and color; instead, look for printers with a separate cartridge for each color. In printers with combined cartridges, you have to dump the whole cartridge as soon as one color runs out, and this can quickly become expensive.

In addition, printers do not always come supplied with the cable required to connect them to your computer. This is just a one-time cost, but something worth checking before you make your purchase.

Photo printers: a buyer's guide

Resolution

As with so many things in the world of digital photography, resolution is the key issue to consider when purchasing an inkjet printer. Some printers are able to output very high-quality images at resolutions of 1,440 dpi or even 2,880 dpi. These high resolutions may sound too high for your needs when you're working on images of only 300 pixels per inch, but remember that inkjet printers work with patterns of tiny dots to represent a single color at photo quality. Don't try to change the resolution of your images to 1,440 ppi to match, however. An 8 x 10-inch (20 x 25 cm) shot would be almost 200 Mb in size.

Paper

When purchasing an inkjet printer, remember that it is important to first consider the size of the print that you intend to output. Most printers print to standard 8½ x 11-inch (22 x 28 cm) letter size. This is ideal for most users' needs, but if you wish to print at the larger 11 x 17-inch (28 x 43 cm) size, there are a number of relatively inexpensive large-format printers on the market that offer impressive results.

Quality and speed

Printers will quote high numbers of pages per minute, but you will find these timings very disappointing when printing photos. Inkjets will have numerous quality settings, each one a trade-off between the result and the time it takes. If you plan to make a lot of photo-quality prints, look for a fast machine.

Margins

Most printers cannot print all the way to the edge of a page, which can be quite disappointing, especially if you want to produce traditional 4 x 6-inch (10 x 15 cm) prints. If you think you will want to use the whole page, look for an "edge-to-edge printing" feature.

Paper feed tray
Check to see what size
of paper your printer
can take, and how many
sheets fit in the feeder.

Card reader
Some printers have
a slot to take the
digital media cards
directly from your
camera, without the
need for a PC.

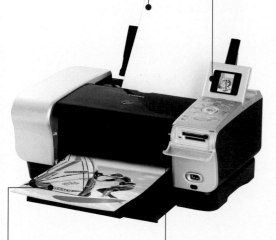

Paper path
Check the route that
paper will take through
your printer. A straight
path allows you to use
thicker paper than printers
that take the paper
through small rollers.

Print head
The most complicated
part of your printer is the
head, which travels back
and forth over the page,
spraying controlled drops
of ink. The more nozzles,
the better the quality is
likely to be.

▶ **JARGON BUSTER**

How many colors do you need in an inkjet?

Early inkjets were able to print in only four colors: cyan,
magenta, yellow, and black. Because most colors can be
created using a blend of these four inks, this allowed
users to print out good-quality photographs. Today's
inkjets have added more colors into the mix—some
come equipped with up to seven different colors of ink.

The addition of lighter versions of cyan and
magenta, as well as a gray ink cartridge, has improved
the output quality, which now rivals that of traditional
film printing. In general, the more colors that your
inkjet features, the greater the quality of the printout
will be—remember, though, that extra colors will mean
greater expense when it comes to purchasing your
replacement ink cartridges.

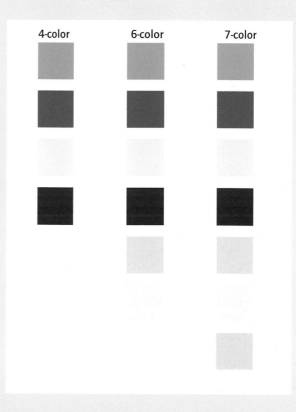

Printer controls

Many printers come equipped with preinstalled drivers. A driver is a specially designed piece of software that allows you to connect your printer to your home computer and output images. Some types of drivers offer additional functionality and control over the sort of print that you are able to output. Here we examine the range of controls available.

From the *File* menu in most software applications, selecting *Print* will bring up the *Print* dialog box. This allows access to a range of basic and advanced printer controls. By far the most important setting to specify is the paper size. Failure to do this may result in your printer outputting an image on the wrong size paper—an expensive mistake to make if you are using photo-quality paper. Because different papers need different methods of printing, it is just as important to select the correct paper type from the pop-up menu.

▶ JARGON BUSTER

What is ColorSync?

Many drivers allow you to adjust the printer's color settings. This is a complicated task even for professionals. Apple's operating system, for example, includes ColorSync, which is a color management system that automatically ensures that your photographs are printed with realistic-looking colors.

Windows users with Photoshop Elements can switch on color management by clicking *Edit > Color Settings* in the main menu, but it is safer to leave this turned off and rely on the printer's own software.

Page Setup and *Print Preview*

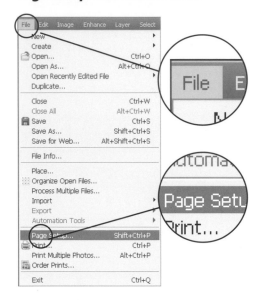

1 The first thing to do when you are ready to print is to set up the page, using the *Page Setup* option found in the *File* menu of most applications.

4 Elements' *Print* function can be found in the *File* menu. This gives you an all-in-one window where you can see a preview, scale the image, and set many other options for printing your photos.

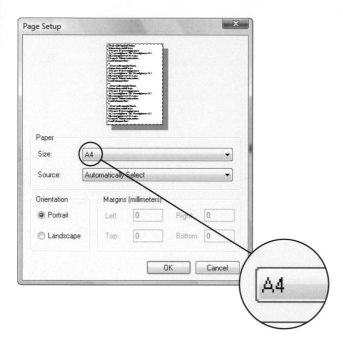

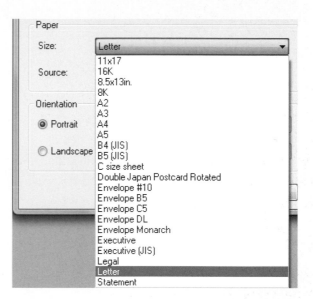

3 Here is a typical range of paper sizes available in an Epson print driver.

2 *Page Setup* enables you to specify the type of printer you're using and the paper size.

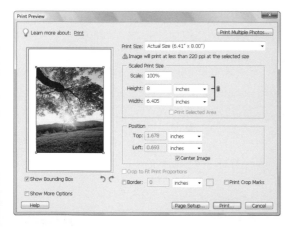

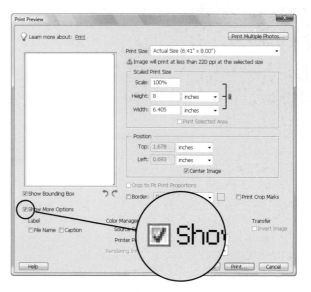

5 The *Print Preview* displays the overall page size, as well as the size of the picture being printed. It allows you to scale the photograph (larger or smaller) and alter its position on the page.

6 Using the *Show More Options* button enables you to add elements such as captions and crop marks.

continued . . .

Printer controls—continued

7 The *Print* dialog panel gives you various output options, including the number of copies you wish to print.

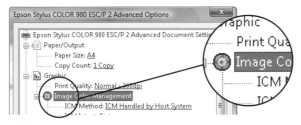

9 Depending on your software, you may get the opportunity to select *Color Management* at this point. If you do so, your image editor will embed a color profile with the image, which tells the printer how the colors looked on your screen *(see pages 24–25)*. If your printer understands this information, it will use it to try and reproduce the colors more exactly. Be warned, though: sometimes the results don't look as good as leaving the management off. You can only find out how successful it is for your hardware by trying it once turned on and once turned off.

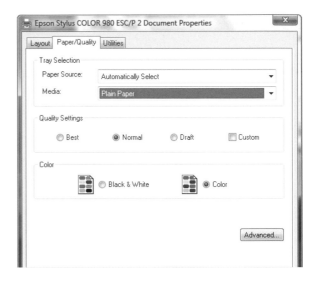

8 If you print to two or more types of paper, check that you have selected the right one.

10 Finally, sit back and wait while your printer works. Remember to wait a few moments for the ink to dry before picking up the results, especially when using glossy papers.

Paper

To get the best results from your inkjet printer, it is essential to use good-quality paper. Printer manufacturers usually offer a range of papers designed specifically to work with their printers. These papers allow you to output anything from a simple gloss or matte photograph to a high-quality textured greeting card.

There is a huge variety of different papers available, ranging in quality from standard lightweight copy paper through to ultrafine glossy photo paper. Before you purchase paper, it is advisable that you have a clear idea of what you intend to do with your printed photograph. Different types of photographs require different types of paper—a small snapshot, for example, will not require expensive gloss photo-quality paper; similarly, an image destined to be hung in a frame will not look good printed on low-grade copy paper.

Purchasing paper

In general, the less expensive papers cannot compete with the pricier high-quality ones. Glossy papers will produce prints with greater contrast and brightness— ideal for framing behind glass. Matte papers, on the other hand, can add an artistic feel to a photograph. Some companies offer less expensive types of paper, which they claim can be used in any inkjet printer. Be careful when using these, though—the results may be acceptable, but be aware that manufacturers often design their papers to work hand in hand with their own print mechanisms and inks. There is also a slight risk that some of the thicker papers could damage your printer.

Cartridges

Here again, it is recommended that you use the inks sold by the manufacturer for use with your particular printer model. Although cheaper cartridges are available, these do not always produce the same results or last for the same amount of time without fading. Note that some manufacturers supply standard color cartridges and special "photo-color" cartridges for the same printer. Use the latter if you want to ensure the best results.

Pictures and frames

Framing a photograph can make or break an image. A good-quality frame complements and enhances a picture without distracting the viewer's attention. Unfortunately, good-quality frames can be expensive to purchase. With an image-editing program such as Adobe Photoshop Elements, however, it is easy to make your own digital frame.

Many frames already come with a mount—this is usually a piece of card with a rectangular hole that rests between the picture and the glass. You can, however, achieve a similar effect on your home computer. To do this, simply add a colored edge to your print. More sophisticated borders can be created using the painting tools available in most image-editing software programs. There are also additional programs on the market, such as PhotoFrame by Extensis, specifically designed for creating frames.

Digital frames

1 This dramatic desert landscape will benefit from adding an equally dramatic frame to set it off.

4 Select the image layer and use the *Magic Wand* tool to select the area outside the image. Then switch to the top (blank) layer and fill that selection with white.

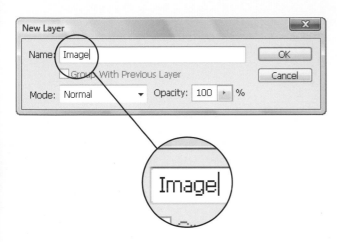

2 Begin adding your frame by giving the image its own layer. You can do this by double-clicking on the background layer in the *Layers* palette—name this layer "Image."

3 Delete the background and create a new empty layer. Name this layer "Frame" and move it by clicking and dragging so the main image is sandwiched between the two empty layers you have created.

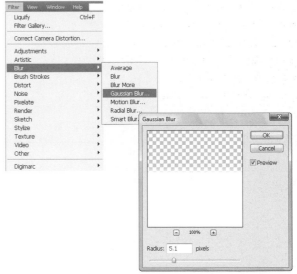

5 Zoom out of the image and use the *Transform* tool to scale the white frame beyond the area of the image.

6 Blur the frame a little using the *Gaussian Blur* filter. The amount of blur that you use will depend on the size of your image—a 5-pixel blur, for example, will look very different on a 5-megapixel image compared to how it would look on a 1-megapixel image.

continued . . .

Pictures and frames—continued

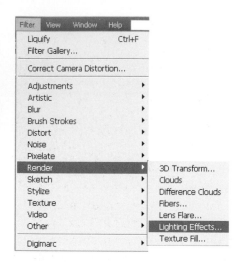

7 Return to the *Filter* menu and select the *Lighting Effects* filter from the *Render* sub-menu to give the frame a three-dimensional appearance.

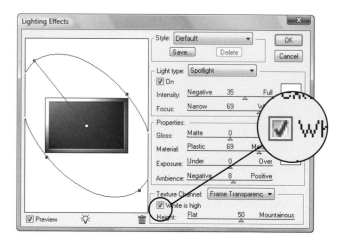

8 In *Lighting Effects,* click on the *Texture Channel* and select *Frame Transparency*. Ensure that the "White is high" check box is selected. In the preview window, the frame will now appear gray and three-dimensional. Experiment with the lights by clicking and dragging their handles until you are satisfied with the results.

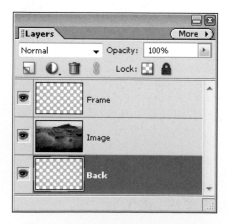

11 Here the *Hue/Saturation* has been applied as an adjustment layer.

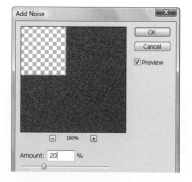

12 Next, add some texture to the frame using the *Add Noise* filter from the *Filter* menu.

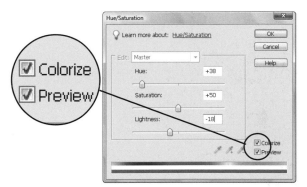

10 Use the *Hue/Saturation* control to add color to the frame. Make sure that the *Frame* layer is selected and check the *Colorize* button in the dialog box. Using these three controls, it is possible to make your frame any color.

9 This shows the lighting effect applied to the plain white frame border. Select the background layer, then use the *Paint Bucket* tool to fill it with white.

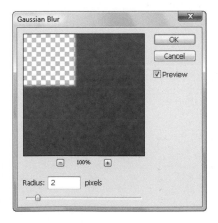

13 Use a *Gaussian Blur* (*Filter > Blur > **Gaussian Blur...***) to subtly soften the noise effect.

14 Select the *Text* tool and add a caption to your photograph to complete the overall effect.

Basic greeting cards

Using image-editing software, it is possible to create your own greeting cards—a personal touch sure to surprise and please your family and friends.

Even the most basic image-editing software has all the tools required to make professional-looking greeting cards. The central element of a personalized card is the photograph you select. Also important are the style and feel of the card—this is generally dictated by the text and typeface that accompanies a design. A classic typeface such as Times, for example, would not be appropriate for a humorous card, where a more cartoonlike font would work better.

In this exercise Adobe Photoshop Elements is used to create a personalized birthday card for a motorcycle enthusiast. You may adopt these techniques to create a variety of different cards for every occasion.

▶ PICTURE PERFECT

Keep it simple

Less is more when it comes to designing a greeting card. Limit the number of fonts, avoid wild colors and impressive filters, and minimize the number of images you use to create cards with the greatest impact.

Personalizing a greeting

1 The first step in designing your card is to select a suitable image. This macho road hog is ideal.

3 Paste the selection into the new document.

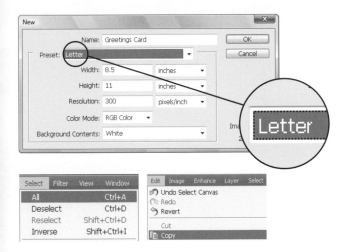

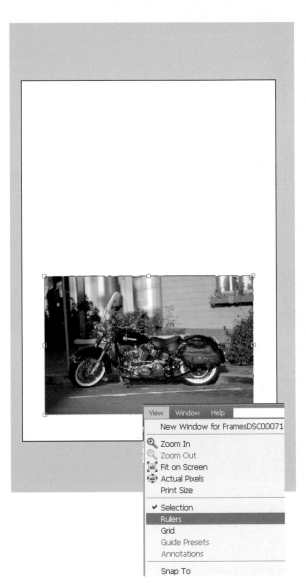

2 Create a new document that is the same size as the card you wish to print–in this case letter size. Open the image you have chosen for the card and *Select All*. Copy the selection and switch to your new document.

4 Use the *Free Transform* tool to scale the image so that it fits comfortably into the new document. Zoom out so that you can see the image's bounding box in full.

5 Scale down the selection using the handles. Hold down the *Shift* key to keep the proportions correct. Make *Rulers* visible to help guide and place your image and the other items you'll be using to make your card.

continued . . .

Basic greeting cards—continued

6 Select the *Line Tool* from the *Tools* palette. Using the *Rulers* as a guide, draw a line along the middle of the page where the card will later be folded.

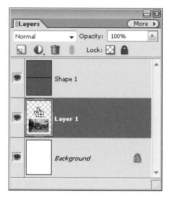

7 Control-click on the project image's thumbnail in the *Layers* palette to load its *Transparency* selection. This places a marquee around the picture.

9 The *Stroke* command draws a line along the edge of your selection. It has a number of options that control the width of the stroke, color, and placement. Choose one to suit your image.

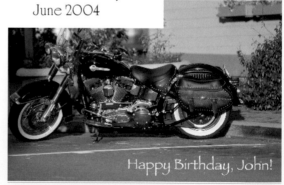

10 Use the *Text* tool to add some text. Here we have added a greeting on the front of the card and personalized text on the back.

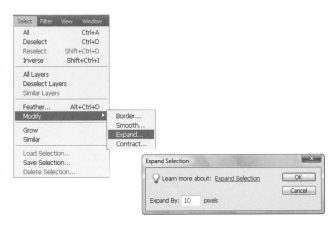

Harley Davidson, California
for John's Birthday
June 2004

(8) Use the *Modify* command to make the selection slightly larger than the picture.

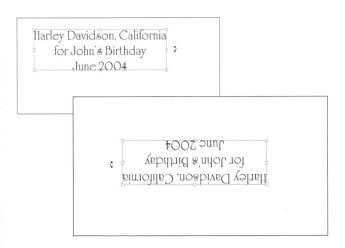

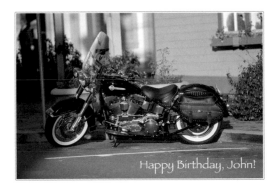

(11) At this point the text will be upside down when the card is printed. Use the *Free Transform* tool to rotate the text. Holding down the *Shift* key as you rotate the text will lock the text to exact right angles.

(12) Here is the finished card with both the image and text in place. Note that the text at the top may look wrong on the screen, but it will fall into place when you print and fold the card.

Passport photos

Doing your own photo printing isn't just about printing snaps—it also offers practical benefits. The "passport photos" used for ID cards and membership cards, for example, can easily be created at home, saving you both time and expense. Here's how to do it.

First a word of warning. Some organizations, especially government bodies like the passport office, only accept purpose-made prints such as those from a photo booth. Do remember to obey the rules of the agency in question. These will probably include using a white background, not wearing hats, caps, or sunglasses, and ensuring even contrast in the image. This is unlikely to be a problem with a local club, however.

Have fun!

This printing technique is not limited to producing passport photos. Feel free to experiment a little. If you copy four different photos onto the *Canvas*, for example, you will have a nice little image collection, perfect for framing. Alternatively, take the same basic photo and give each copy a different filter or color treatment. The results can look really great.

Creating multiple images

1 A "passport" type picture is, roughly speaking, 1⅜ x 1¾ inches (35 x 45 mm)—so set the controls of your *Crop* tool to that dimension at a decent printing resolution. Then crop your image accordingly—the type of image you pick will depend on the purpose of the picture.

4 Double-click on your single layer to make it a floating layer instead of the background. Name your new layer, calling it something you will be able to quickly identify later.

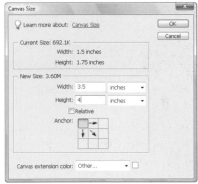

2 Next, make sure that white is selected as your background color (click in the lower colour patch at the bottom of the *Toolbox* if you need to change it) and use the *Erase* tool to erase the background from the image and give you a clean head shot.

3 Resize the *Canvas*, anchoring the picture in the top-left corner.

5 Next, select the new layer, then click on the *Move* tool. Holding the *Alt* and *Shift* keys, drag the layer to the right. Holding *Alt* as you drag creates a copy layer, and *Shift* makes it follow a straight line. Repeat twice to make four images.

6 Add a little *Drop Shadow* from the *Layer Styles* palette to help the images stand out. Repeat for the remaining layers.

Bookmarks

There are hundreds of interesting ways to use digital photos. This bookmark is just one example. Keep in mind that you are not limited to printing on paper. Most inkjet printers can handle light card stock as well. You can also buy sheets of labels, business cards, stickers, and even T-shirt transfers to transform your favorite shots into something really special. There are also kits available to create refrigerator magnets, mobiles, and window displays. Check with your office supply store for other ideas, and let your imagination run wild.

Printing posters

Your local print shop may have other great ideas for your digital snaps. For instance, many will now blow up your favorite shots to poster size and print them on a special large-format printer. Simply give them the file on a memory card or CD-ROM.

Personalizing work with the *Text* tool

1 This glowing seascape can be used to make a one-of-a-kind bookmark, but first it needs to be cropped.

Brooke's Book!

3 Now select the *Text* tool, select a suitable font, and type in your text at an appropriate size.

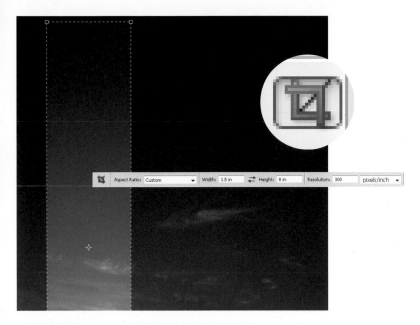

2 Select the *Crop* tool and set it to the size you want. Here, it is 1½ inches (3 cm) wide x 8 inches (20 cm) high at 300 dpi—just right. Move the *Crop* marquee to the best portion of the shot and crop.

4 Make the text more exciting by adding a *Layer Style*. Make sure the *Text* layer is selected and go to the *Layer Styles* palette from the menu, then experiment with the options.

5 Finally, double-click on the *Text* layer, highlight the text in the dialog box, and click on the *Color Picker* (the colored square in the *Options Bar*) to change the color—this gold is perfect.

Emailing your snaps

Sending photographs by email is a fast and easy way to share your images, allowing you to quickly deliver your photographs anywhere in the world. Before you start emailing, however, there are several important points to remember.

Most digital cameras are designed to take pictures that will eventually be printed on photo-quality paper. To achieve a good-quality print, the resolution of the image needs to be high, which requires a larger file size. Larger files, however, take more time to email—and more time for the person at the other end to view. Fortunately, images that are only meant to be viewed on a computer screen do not need to have such a high resolution.

Using image-editing software, it is very easy to reduce the resolution of a picture and its file size—making the image smaller and thus able to be sent and received more quickly. Almost all image-editing programs have a fast option that can handle all of this for you. This option is usually entitled *Save for Web* or *Email Image*.

The Email wizard

Adobe Photoshop Elements provides a speedy method of ensuring that your emailed photographs do not take too long to download. Selecting the *E-mail* option from the *Share* menu on the *Shortcuts Bar* opens up a wizard (through the Organizer). From here you can add or remove images, select the recipients, and even create a message to accompany the photos. There are also options to automatically optimize the size and quality, create a self-contained PDF slide show, or manually set the size and quality for individual attachments. Finally, it will put them all together in a new message using your default E-mail program.

Keep a copy

Whenever you create an email image, be sure to keep a copy of your original picture. Avoid scaling down the sole version of a photograph, since the image will then be suitable only for viewing on a computer screen and you won't be able to print it out to a satisfactory quality.

Preparing photos to email

1 Although Adobe Photoshop Elements features the *E-Mail wizard*, you can achieve a greater degree of control by saving the file yourself. To create the best-looking image at the smallest file size, it is best to select *Save for Web* from the *File* menu.

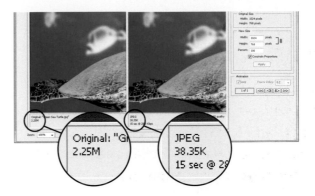

2 The *Save for Web* dialog box *(above)* allows you to see how an image will look when reduced. The figures beneath the windows—before *(left)* and after *(right)*—display the file size. The after window also tells you how long it will take to download the photo. This image, for example, will take 22 seconds to download on a slow Internet connection.

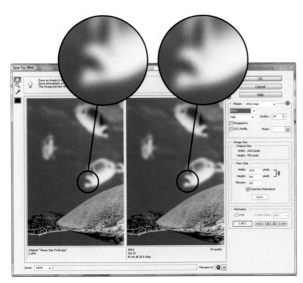

3 You can adjust any of the settings and instantly see the effect on the image and the file size. Here the JPEG quality setting has been changed to *Low* (*Quality* 10). The file size is now 39.1Kb and the picture will take only 15 seconds to download. You can see, however, that the quality of the image has suffered.

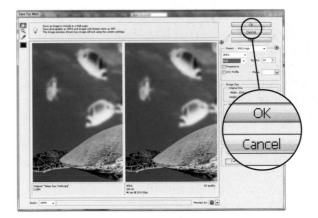

4 Taking the JPEG quality setting up to *High* (*Quality* 60) increases the file size to 117.3Kb; this means that it will take a person with a slow Internet connection some 43 seconds to download. When you have finished adjusting the settings, click the *OK* button to save your photograph in its smaller, more email-friendly form.

Slide shows

You can create the modern equivalent of a slide show with just your digital camera and a home computer. For greater impact you can even add your own soundtrack and picture captions.

Many image-editing software programs include a slide show feature. Some programs are more sophisticated than others, featuring additional creative options, such as adding fades and dissolves to transitions between photographs. Even if your image-editing software is more basic, it is still possible for you to create an impressive slide show.

▶ **PICTURE PERFECT**

Telling a story
Think of your slide show as a short movie, with a beginning, middle, and end. Keep in mind that if you can't get excited looking at your own slide show, you can't expect anybody else to. So be sure to arrange the order of your images so that they tell a story. Providing captions for your photographs can help you achieve this, as can the addition of a soundtrack. If you decide to include a soundtrack, make sure it complements rather than distracts from your photographs.

iPhoto slide shows
Apple's free image-editing software iPhoto features an excellent slide show facility, which allows you to take selected images as well as add a soundtrack to create your own slide show quickly and easily. iPhoto gives you control over the timing of your photographs and the option of displaying your images either onscreen or on any tv that is connected to your home computer.

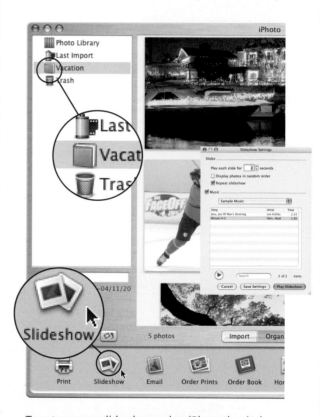

To set up your slide show using iPhoto, begin by selecting any photo album you want to show from the right-hand column and click the *Slideshow* button.

Then decide on the duration of each slide. The final step is to add the music by making selections from your iTunes library. iTunes is a music catalog, a little like iPhoto, that is also included with Mac OS X.

Adobe Photoshop Elements slide shows

If you own a PC, you can use image-cataloging software such as Photoshop Elements Organizer to create your slide shows.

The Organizer has a built-in slide show function. Simply select the *Slide show* option from the *Create* menu on the *Shortcuts Bar.*

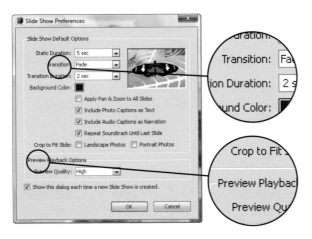

From there you are taken to a wizard that allows you to specify individual settings, such as the transition, style, and speed. You can then choose to add or remove photos from the show.

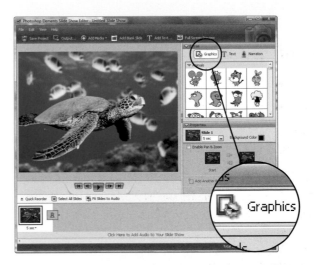

The wizard lets you personalize the slide show further by allowing you to add clip art, text, and even narration and music if you wish.

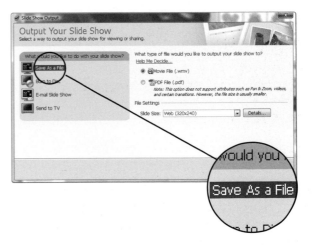

Now you're ready to sit back and enjoy the show. Elements lets you run a preview to check the slide show. It also gives you the option of saving to a movie file or PDF document for e-mailing. You can also burn it to a CD or DVD, which can be viewed on a standard DVD player.

Click!

Putting photos on the Web

One of the most exciting ways to share your photographs with other people is to make your very own art gallery on the Web. This is advantageous since it allows you to exhibit your photographs to a worldwide audience. Not so long ago this would have been a complicated task to undertake, but modern image-editing software packages now make it easy to create your own Web gallery—you can have everything up and running within minutes of taking your photographs.

To create your own gallery, you must first have an account with an Internet Service Provider (ISP). Before starting work, check that your account offers Web space—without Web space you will be unable to display your photographs on-line. Prepare your photographs using image-editing software such as Adobe Photoshop Elements—this program breaks the process of Web gallery creation into simple, easy-to-follow steps. The following example demonstrates just how straightforward it is to create a Web gallery.

Uploading your photographs

A word of warning: when you have finished preparing your images, you will need to upload them to your Web space. Before attempting this, you may wish to contact your Internet Service Provider (ISP) to establish the correct procedure for uploading photographs—individual ISPs often vary in their methods of uploading images.

Web photo gallery

Publishing on the Internet is made very easy by wizards. The hardest part is probably choosing which images to share with the world.

1 Collect all the images that you want people to see on your Web gallery, and then save them in one folder on your computer. It doesn't matter what size they are.

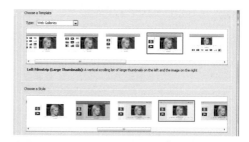

3 You can now define the appearance of your Web gallery. At the very top of the window you have the template options. You can choose from standard web galleries, animated slideshows, and even interactive displays. Choosing the Web Galleries gives a second window, where colored and textured styles can be applied to give extra appeal. Click the *Next Step* button and Elements will generate the necessary pages and files.

2 In Photoshop Elements, click *File > Create > Photo Galleries*. This opens the Photo Galleries wizard. Begin by clicking the *Add* button to select the folder of photos you have just prepared. You can also select images from the Organizer itself.

As well as creating your own gallery, there are a number of alternatives. Flickr (www.flickr.com), for example, is a community photo-sharing site used by thousands of people. Apple's .Mac Internet service allows iPhoto users to upload their albums. Adobe has its own site, Photoshop Showcase, where you can upload and share your galleries straight from Elements.

▶ **JARGON BUSTER**

FTP

If your ISP gives you web space with a File Transfer Protocol (FTP) address to upload your files to, you'll find it easier than you think. Many people believe you need a dedicated FTP program on your computer, but instead you can type the address into Microsoft Internet Explorer (and some other web browsers) just like a Web address. Just add ftp:// before the address, instead of http://. A typical server address is ftp://ftp.yourisp.com/yourspace. You will probably have to fill in a pop-up with your account number and password. Check the details with your provider.

Once the formalities have been completed, you will be presented with file windows much like those in your computer's operating system. They'll be a bit slower, but you will still be able to drag and drop to copy a file onto the Internet.

4 Once your Web gallery has been built, you can add text, tweak the display, optimize for faster downloading, and preview the finished article; this can be done either in the wizard's window or in your web browser. Finally you can choose how and where to share the gallery. This can be to your web space via FTP (see opposite), onto a CD to mail to someone, or uploaded to the Adobe Photoshop Showcase site.

Glossary

Adobe Inc
Software developer whose products are widely used by professionals and amateurs for many creative tasks such as web design, graphic design, and video editing. Photoshop, Photoshop Elements, and the graphic-design package InDesign are some of its most successful products.

alpha channel
While each color channel defines the level of a certain color for each pixel, this channel defines the level of transparency for each pixel, allowing you to create images with objects of varying levels of transparency.

anti-aliasing
The smoothing of jagged edges on diagonal lines created in an imaging program, by giving intermediate values to pixels between the steps. This is especially common around text.

application
Software designed to make the computer perform a specific task. For example, Photoshop is an image-editing application, whereas Windows is an operating system.

artifact
Any flaw in a digital image, such as "noise." Most artifacts are undesirable, although adding "noise" can create a desirable grainy texture in an appropriate image.

backup
A copy of either a file or a program created in case the original file becomes damaged (corrupt) or lost.

bit depth
The number of bits per pixel (usually per channel, sometimes for all the channels combined), which determines the number of colors that pixel can display. Eight bits per channel are needed for photographic-quality imaging.

bitmapped graphic
An image made up of dots, or pixels, such as those produced by digital cameras, scanners, and software like Photoshop. It is distinct from the vector images of "object-oriented" drawing applications.

browser/web browser
Program that enables the viewing or "browsing" of World Wide Web pages across the Internet. The most widely used browsers are Microsoft Internet Explorer, Firefox, and Safari (Mac only).

burn(ing)
The act of recording data onto a CD or DVD using a CD or DVD burner (these are supplied with most new computers).

byte
Eight bits. The basic data unit of desktop computing.

CCD
(Charged Coupled Device) The name given to the component of a digital camera which "sees" and records the images, like film does in a traditional camera. The CCD is made up of a grid of tiny light sensors, one for each pixel. The number of sensors, and the size of image output by the CCD, is measured in megapixels.

CD-ROM
Compact Disc Read-Only Memory. An evolution of the CD that allows the storage of up to 600 megabytes of data, such as images, video clips, text, and other digital files. But the discs are "Read only," which means the user can't edit or overwrite the data.

CD-R/CD-RW CD
Recordable/CD-ReWriteable. CD-Rs are inexpensive discs on which you can store any digital data, or roughly 77 minutes of audio (on a hi-fi CD recorder). But once written and finalized (fixed), the data cannot be erased, edited, or modified. Similar to the above, CD-RW discs can be "unfinalized" then overwritten, in part or entirely, any number of times. However, CD-RWs will not play on all CD drives, so they are primarily used for storage.

channel
Images are commonly described in terms of channels, which can be viewed as a sheet of color similar to a layer. Commonly, a color image will have a channel allocated to each primary color (red, green, and blue in a standard RGB image) and sometimes an alpha channel for transparency, or even an additional channel for professional printing with special inks.

clone/cloning
In most image-editing packages, clone tools allow the user to sample pixels (picture elements) from one part of an image, such as a digital photograph, and use them to "paint" over another area of the image. This process is often used for the removal of unwanted parts of an image or correcting problems, such as facial blemishes. In Photoshop, the tool is called the *Clone Stamp* tool (sometimes known as the rubber stamp).

CMYK
The standard primary colors used by professional, or "process," printing: cyan, magenta, yellow, and key (black). These colors are mixed according to "subtractive color," meaning that white appears where no color value is applied.

color depth
See *bit depth.*

color gamut
The range of color that can be produced by an output device, such as a printer or a computer monitor.

color picker
An onscreen palette of colors used to describe and define the colors displayed and used in an application or on a computer monitor. Color pickers may be specific to an application such as Adobe Photoshop, a third-party color system such as PANTONE, or to the operating system running on your computer.

compression
The technique of rearranging data so that it either occupies less space on a disc or transfers faster between devices or over communication lines. For example, high-quality digital images, such as photographs, can take up an enormous amount of disc space, transfer slowly, and use a lot of processing power. They need to be compressed (the file size needs to be made smaller) before they can be published on the web, otherwise they take too long to appear on screen. But compressing them can lead to a loss of quality. Compression methods that do not lose data are referred to as "lossless," while "lossy" describes methods in which some data is lost.

continuous-tone image
An image, such as a photograph, in which there is a smooth progression of tones from black to white.

contrast
The degree of difference between adjacent tones in an image from the lightest to the darkest. "High

contrast" describes an image with light highlights and dark shadows, but few shades in between, while a "low contrast" image is one with even tones and few dark areas or highlights.

copyright
The right of a person who creates an original work to protect that work by controlling how and where it may be reproduced.

copyright-free
A misnomer used to describe ready-made resources, such as clip art. In fact, these resources are rarely, if ever, "copyright free." Generally it is only the license to use the material that is granted by purchase. "Royalty free" is a more accurate description, as you don't have to pay per copy used.

digitize
To convert anything—text, images, or sound—into binary form so that it can be digitally processed. In other words, transforming analog data (a traditional photograph or an audio tape, for example) into digital data.

dithering
A technique by which a large range of colors can be simulated by mingling pixels. A complex pattern of intermingling adjacent pixels of two colors gives the illusion of a third color, although this makes the image appear grainy.

dots per inch
(dpi) A unit of measurement used to represent the resolution of output devices such as printers and also, erroneously, monitors and images, whose resolution should be expressed in pixels per inch (ppi). The closer the dots or pixels (the more there are to each inch) the better the quality.

Typical resolutions are 72 ppi for a monitor, 600 dpi for a laser printer, and 1,440 dpi for an inkjet printer.

download
To transfer data from a remote computer, such as an Internet server, to your own. The opposite of upload.

DVD
(Digital Versatile Disc). Similar in appearance to CDs and CD-ROMs, but with a much greater storage capacity. Although store-bought movie DVDs hold up to 18 Gb, you can only burn around 4-5 Gb on the various home formats. Like CD-R and CD-RW you can buy blank discs that can be written once or re-written repeatedly. Unlike CDs, however, there are competing formats that look the same but cannot write to each other's discs. These are DVD-R/RW, DVD+R/RW, and DVD-RAM. When buying blank discs be sure to choose the correct sort. The write-once discs from both DVD-R and DVD+R can be read by most modern DVD players, so with the correct software, you can make DVDs of photo slide shows or digital videos at home.

EPS
(Encapsulated PostScript) Image file format for object-oriented graphics, as in drawing programs and page-layout programs.

extract
A process in many image-editing applications whereby a selected part of an image is removed from areas around it. Typically, a subject is "extracted" from the background.

eyedropper tool
In applications such as Photoshop and Photoshop Elements, a tool for gauging or selecting the color of pixels.

file extension
The term for the abbreviated suffix at the end of a file name that describes either its type (such as .eps or .jpg) or origin (the application that created it, such as .qxp for QuarkXPress files). Extensions are compulsory and essentially automatic in Windows, but not on Apple computers, so Mac users should add them if they want their files to work on Windows computers.

file format
The way a program arranges data so that it can be stored or displayed on a computer. Common file formats include TIFF (.tif) and JPEG (.jpg) for bitmapped image files, EPS (.eps) for object-oriented image files, and ASCII (.txt) for text files.

FireWire
A type of port connection that allows for high-speed transfer of data between a computer and peripheral devices. Also known as IEEE-1394 or iLink, this method of transfer—quick enough for digital video—is employed by some high-resolution cameras to move data faster than USB.

frame
A single still picture from a movie or animation sequence. Also a single complete image from a TV picture.

font
Set of characters sharing the same typeface, these are stored by your computer and made available to applications where text is edited. There are two kinds of font—vector fonts like TrueType or OpenType which can be printed at any size with no loss of quality, and bitmapped fonts which cannot be scaled.

Gb
(GigaByte) Approximately one billion bytes (actually 1,073,741,824), or 1024 megabytes.

GIF
(Graphics Interchange Format) A bitmapped image format commonly used on the Internet. GIF is a 256-color format with two specifications, GIF8a and GIF89a, the latter providing additional features such as the use of transparent backgrounds. The GIF format uses a "lossless" compression technique, which handles areas of similar color well, and allows animation. It is therefore a common format for graphics and logos on the Internet, but JPEG is preferred for photographs.

gradation/gradient
The smooth transition from one color or tone to another. Photoshop and other programs include a Gradient tool to create these transitions automatically.

histogram
A "map" of the distribution of tones in an image, arranged as a graph. The horizontal axis is in 256 steps from black to white (or dark to light), and the vertical axis is the number of pixels, so in a dark image you'll find taller bars in the darker shades.

HSL
(Hue, Saturation, Lightness.) A way of representing colors based upon the way that colors are transmitted from a TV screen or monitor. The hue is the pure color from the spectrum, the saturation is the intensity of the color pigment (without black or white added), and brightness representing the strength of luminance from light to dark (the amount of black or

white present). Variously called HLS (hue, lightness, saturation), HSV (hue, saturation, value) and HSB (hue, saturation, brightness).

hue
A color found in its pure state in the spectrum.

icon
An onscreen graphical representation of an object (such as a disc, file, folder or tool), used to make identification and selection easier.

interface
A term used to describe the screen design that links the user with the computer program or website. The quality of the user interface often determines how well users will be able to navigate their way around the pages within the site.

interpolation
Bitmapping procedure used in resizing an image to maintain resolution. When the number of pixels is increased, interpolation fills in the gaps by comparing the values of adjacent pixels.

ISP
(Internet Service Provider) An organization that provides access to the Internet. At its most basic this may be a telephone number for connection, but most ISPs provide email addresses and web space for new sites.

JPEG, JPG
The Joint Photographic Experts Group. An ISO (International Standards Organization) group that defines compression standards for bitmapped color images. The abbreviated form gives its name to a "lossy" (meaning some data may be lost) compressed file format in which the degree of compression, ranging from high compression and

low quality, to low compression and high quality, can be defined by the user.

Kb
(kilobyte) Approximately one thousand bytes (actually 1,024).

lasso
A selection tool used to draw an outline around an area.

layer
One level of an image file, separate from the rest, allowing different elements to be moved and edited in much the same way as animators draw onto sheets of transparent acetate.

lossless/lossy
Refers to the data-losing qualities of different compression methods. "Lossless" means that no image information is lost; "lossy" means that some (or much) of the image data is lost in the compression process (but the data will download more quickly).

luminosity
Brightness of color. This does not affect the hue or color saturation.

mask
A grayscale template that hides part of an image. One of the most important tools in editing an image, it is used to make changes to a limited area. In Photoshop Elements a mask can only be applied to an adjustment layer, but in Photoshop masks can be applied to all layers.

MB
(megabyte) Approximately one million bytes (actually 1,048,576).

megapixel
This has become the typical measure of the resolution of a digital camera's

CCD. It is simply the number of pixels on the CCD, so a size of 1280 x 960 pixels is equal to 1228800 pixels, or 1.2 megapixels.

memory card
The media employed by a digital camera to save photos on. This can be Compact Flash, Memory Stick, SD Cards or Smart Media— all store images which can then be transferred to the computer.

menu
An on-screen list of choices available to the user.

midtones/middletones
The range of tonal values in an image anywhere between the darkest and lightest, usually referring to those approximately halfway.

noise
Random pattern of small spots on a digital image that are generally unwanted, caused by non-image-forming electrical signals. Noise is a type of artifact.

pixel
(picture element) The smallest component of any digitally generated image. In its simplest form, one pixel corresponds to a single bit: 0 = off, or white, and 1 = on, or black. In color or grayscale images or monitors, one pixel may correspond to several bits. An 8-bit pixel, for example, can be displayed in any of 256 colors, a 24-bit pixel (8 bits per channel) can display any one of 16.8 million colors.

pixels per inch
(ppi) A measure of resolution for a bitmapped image.

plug-in
Subsidiary software for a browser or other package that enables it to

perform additional functions, e.g., play sound, movies or video.

PNG
(Portable Network Graphics) A file format for images used on the Web, which provides 10–30% "lossless" compression, or a "lossy" option. It was created as an alternative to the GIF and JPG file formats, but has not yet displaced either.

RAM
(Random Access Memory) The working memory of a computer, to which the central processing unit (CPU) has direct, immediate access. The data here is only stored while the computer is switched on, and more RAM can dramatically improve a computer's performance.

raster(ization)
Deriving from the Latin word "rastrum," meaning "rake," this is the method of displaying (and creating) images on a television or computer screen. It is commonly used to mean the conversion of a scaleable vector graphics image into a bitmapped image.

resolution
(1) The degree of quality, definition or clarity with which an image is reproduced or displayed, for example in a photograph, or via a scanner, monitor screen, printer, or other output device.

resolution
(2) monitor resolution, screen resolution. The number of pixels across by pixels down. Common resolutions are 640 x 480, 800 x 600 and 1,024 x 768, with 800 x 600 the size most web designers plan for.

re-sampling
Changing the resolution of an image either by removing pixels

(so lowering the resolution) or adding them by interpolation (so increasing the resolution).

RGB
(Red, Green, Blue) The primary colors of the "additive" color model, used in video technology, computer monitors and for graphics such as for the Web and multimedia.

ROM
(Read-Only Memory) Memory, such as on a CD-ROM, which can only be read, not written to. It retains its contents without power, unlike RAM.

Rubber stamp
Another word for a clone tool (see *cloning*).

software
Programs that enable a computer to perform tasks, from its operating system to job-specific applications such as image-editing programs and third-party filters.

thumbnail
A small representation of an image used mainly for identification purposes in a file browser or, within Photoshop, to illustrate the current status of layers and channels.

TIFF
(Tagged Image File Format) A standard and popular graphics file format originally developed by Aldus (now merged with Adobe) and Microsoft, used for scanned, high-resolution, bitmapped images and for color separations. The TIFF format stores each pixel's color individually, with no compression, at whatever bit depth you choose. That means they can be black and white, grayscale, RGB color or CMYK color, can be read by different computer platforms, but can be very large files. For

example, an image of 640 x 480 pixels (just 0.3 megapixels) at 8 bits per channel CMYK (32 bits per pixel) is 1.2Mb.

tile, tiling
Repeating a graphic item and placing the repetitions side-by-side in all directions so that they form a pattern.

toolbox
In an application, an area of the interface that enables instant access to the most commonly used commands and features. Unless switched off by the user, the toolbox is always visible on screen.

transparency
A degree of transparency applied to a pixel so that, when the image or layer is used in conjunction with others, it can be seen through. Only some file formats allow for transparency, including TIFFs which define transparency as an alpha channel, or GIFs, which allow only absolute transparency (a pixel is either colored or transparent).

TrueType
A type of font or typeface composed of vector graphics which can be scaled up or down without any loss in quality.

USB
(Universal Serial Bus) An interface standard developed to replace the slow, unreliable serial and parallel ports on computers. USB allows devices to be plugged and unplugged while the computer is switched on. It is now the standard means for connecting printers, scanners, and digital cameras.

vector graphics
Images made up of mathematically defined shapes, such as circles and rectangles,

or complex paths built out of mathematically defined curves. Vector graphics images can be displayed at any size or resolution without loss of quality, and are easy to edit because the shapes retain their identity, but they lack the tonal subtlety of bitmapped images. They are used in illustrations for their accuracy and clarity, and employed by Photoshop's text handling and shape tools.

Web page
A published HTML document on the World Wide Web, which when linked with others, forms a website. The HTML code contains text, layout and navigational instructions, plus links to the graphics used on the page.

Web server
A computer ("host") that is dedicated to web services.

Website
The address, location (on a server), and collection of documents and resources for any particular interlinked set of Web pages.

Windows
Operating system for PCs developed by Microsoft using a graphic interface that imitated that of the Macintosh.

World Wide Web
(WWW) The term used to describe the entire collection of web servers all over the world that are connected to the Internet.

Click!

Index

INDEX

Useful websites

Adobe®
The developers of Photoshop and Photoshop Elements, along with other graphics applications.
www.adobe.com

Apple Computer
Manufacturers of Apple iMac, Mac Book, and Mac Pro computers. Developers of OS X, iPhoto, iMovie and more.
www.apple.com

Corel
Graphics software developers, with applications including Paint Shop Pro.
www.corel.com

DP Review
A great online resource for reviews and tips on digital cameras.
www.dpreview.com

ePHOTOzine
An excellent website, with reviews, forums, and ideas.
www.ephotozine.com

Microsoft
Developers of the Windows Operating System and the Picture It! and Image Suite programs.
www.microsoft.com

Web-Linked
Information on more books devoted to digital photography.
www.web-linked.com

Digital camera manufacturers

Fuji
www.fujifilm.com

Olympus
www.olympusamerica.com

Nikon
www.nikon.com

Kodak
www.kodak.com

Canon
www.canon.com

Printer and scanner manufacturers

Epson
www.epson.com

Hewlett Packard
www.hp.com

Lexmark
www.lexmark.com

Canon
www.canon.com